A Unique SOUTHERN OREGON

A Unique
SOUTHERN OREGON

MARGARET LAPLANTE

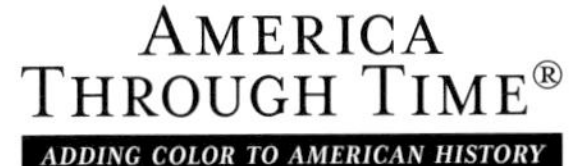

America Through Time is an imprint of Fonthill Media LLC
www.through-time.com
office@through-time.com

Published by Arcadia Publishing by arrangement with Fonthill Media LLC
For all general information, please contact Arcadia Publishing:
Telephone: 843-853-2070
Fax: 843-853-0044
E-mail: sales@arcadiapublishing.com
For customer service and orders:
Toll-Free 1-888-313-2665

www.arcadiapublishing.com

First published 2022

Copyright © Margaret LaPlante 2022

ISBN 978-1-63499-373-9

Typeset in Mrs Eaves XL Serif Narrow
Printed and bound in England

CONTENTS

About the Author

Margaret LaPlante is a historian living in Southern Oregon. She has written many books, magazine articles, and short stories on the history of Oregon.

INTRODUCTION

Just what is it that makes Oregon unique? The first Oregonians, the Indians, found Oregon unique due to the forests, rivers, lakes, natural habitat, and scenic beauty. Long before the first pioneers settled in Oregon, local Indian tribes and bands called this part of the country home. From time to time a fur trapper or explorer would pass through the area, but for the most part they were undisturbed.

Ships would arrive along the Oregon coast. The Indians would sell and trade goods with those vessels. Their furs were always in demand. Captain George Vancouver of the HMS *Discovery* wrote in his journal that the Indians along the Oregon coast were very honest in their trading.

The main staple in the Indian's diet was fish, with acorns, camas, berries, roots, nuts, seeds, plants, and bark rounding out their natural food supply. They would shell acorns then mash them using a mortar and pestle. They would place the mashed acorns on clean sand and pour hot water over them to leach them. That process was repeated, then the mixture was boiled by placing it into a tightly woven basket filled with water and heating it over hot stones. Camas bulbs were dug out of the ground using a long stick, the end of which was sharpened to a point. The bulbs were baked in a pit dug in the ground. Alder bark was placed between the hot stones in the pit and the bulbs. They would cook the bulbs for a day or two until they were roasted, then mash them into cakes and store them for the cold months. Other roots that they consumed included the kice and epars. Wild berries could be eaten fresh or stored for winter. If they were storing the berries for winter, they would boil the berries and then mash them into square cakes. Roots and greens could be dried for the winter months. Hunting for elk, deer, and antelope could provide food for months. Fish and game could be smoked or dried for the long winter months. Along the coast, sea lion, whale, shellfish, clams, and other ocean fish provided meals for the Indians. In some areas of Oregon, the Indians grew tobacco. With that exception they did not need to grow crops due to the availability of what grew naturally. Grasshoppers, insects, small rodents, rabbits, waterfowl, and lizards were also an important part of their diet.

Food items unique to any given area provided an opportunity to trade with other tribes and bands, fur traders, and explorers that passed through the area. Unique items could be traded several times over and sold or traded to coastal tribes and bands who would in turn sell or trade them with ships from around the globe. An example of a unique food item were the wocus seeds from the pond lilies that grew on Klamath Lake. They were dried and eaten locally but also traded with other tribes and bands that did not have access to this particular seed.

The type of houses the Indians lived in depended on the region. Plank houses were the most popular style of a home. When it was time to build a house, they would dig about two feet down along the perimeters of the house. They would erect posts in the corners then use the planks of cedar or sugar pine for the siding. The roofs were made from sugar pine, woven mats, or other natural materials. Most houses had a fire pit that was dug into the earthen floor. The smoke from the fire escaped through small holes they cut in the roof. The door openings were usually round and covered with an animal hide. The Indians wove mats that were used for sleeping and for room partitions. The houses varied in size depending on the number of families who lived in one house. In addition to plank houses, some areas, including the Klamath Lakes, used a circular lodge house. They dug two to six feet in the ground, forming a circle. They erected poles around the circumference and placed mats that they had woven from natural resources all around. Next, they packed hard formed earth all around, creating an earth lodge with a few holes in the roof so that smoke could escape from the fireplace that they built in the center. Willow frame houses were common as well. They used bent willow branches, cottonwood, tule reeds, or sagebrush and covered them with brush and mats. Mat longhouses were another type of house. They were built by placing a series of poles around the structure and covering the structure with mats woven from natural resources. Dirt was piled along the perimeter of the house.

During the warmer months, the Indians would travel to different areas to fish and harvest wild foods that were not available to them locally. When they came across other tribes and bands, they would trade items for things that were not available to them locally. When they traveled, they used woven mats for shelter and bedding. Language barriers could be a problem when they came across other tribes and bands, but they were able to communicate with signs and basic language skills.

Sweat lodges were very important to the Indians. The construction materials varied depending on the region. Some were built using planks of cedar or sugar pine. Others were built with a willow frame covered with mud. Stones were heated and then water was poured over the hot rocks to produce steam. The sweat lodges were used by men for spiritual and healing purposes and for special ceremonies.

The Indians needed canoes in order to fish in the ocean and in rivers and streams. They would hollow out the trunk of a tree using controlled fire. They would then work to shape the canoe using chisels made from large bones or stone. They chose cedar over other woods for its strength and buoyancy, although redwood and fir were also used. They would coat the wood with fish oil or blubber. The canoes varied in size depending on the area and the number of people who would use it at one time. They also built rafts using logs wrapped together with sinew or other natural resources. Poles, paddles, and bailers were crafted from the various woods.

They wove baskets from tree roots, vines, and other natural resources. The baskets were used for food gathering, food preparation, and serving. Some baskets were woven to be watertight and used for cooking. Other baskets were woven in order to carry infants. In some regions the baskets were used for hats and covers. Some of the baskets had a long strap that was worn around the neck, thus freeing the hands for gathering food. They wove various designs into the baskets, which were works of art and prime items for trading.

Fishing nets were made from natural resources that differed from region to region. Seine was a popular choice as was hemp, nettle fiber, and willow. They devised a knotting technique to craft the nets. The nets were constructed based on the type of fish they were seeking. The willow nets were loosely woven into a long, narrow basket. They were used in shallow streams or with a weir. To make weights for the nets, they would drill a hole in a stone using rudimentary tools. The stones were then secured to the net using seine or a similar fiber. In certain areas where there were rapids, falls, or narrow rivers, it was necessary to construct a wooden platform that they could fish off of. In smaller streams they frequently constructed weirs made from logs, rocks, or brush that would slow the fish down enough so that they could catch them in a net or a basket. The Indians also made fishing hooks from bone or wood. Fishing lines were made from sinew or plant fibers. Fishing spears and harpoons were used in shallow water. Fish clubs were made from wood or bone and used to kill the fish.

Bows and arrows were the primary tool used for hunting. The bows were made from whatever wood was available such as oak, juniper, or yew. They built traps and made arrows and spears based on the type of game they were hunting. Snares were built from bent saplings, logs, rocks, and stones. Nets were used to catch certain types of waterfowl. If they were hunting ducks, they sometimes used the skin from a real duck stuffed with tule that the hunter could pull with a string made of sinew or fiber. Sometimes when they were hunting, they would wear a hide from the animal as a disguise. They carried their bow and arrows in a quiver that was made from the hide of an animal.

Tools consisted of bows and arrows, spears, harpoons, animal traps, clubs, grinders, scrapers, wedges, whistles made from hollow bird bones, hammerstones, and mauls. Knives were made from stone or bones. Antlers were used for chopping and splitting. Grinding bowls were made from wood or stone. Pestles were made from stone or other natural resources, depending on the area. Scrapers used on hides were usually made of stone that was pressure flaked on one side to create a sharp side. Drills, awls, and chisels were made from wood or bone. Indians living along the coast would pry metal from ships that wrecked on the rocky shores. They would fashion the metal into tools which were highly sought after in trades with other tribes and bands.

The clothing attire varied from region to region depending on the climate and what natural resources were readily available. Some women wore aprons made of woven mats or braided grass. Some wore knee length skirts of cedar bark. Cedar bark was also used as a shirt. In some regions they wore skins from animals fashioned into a dress or a skirt. In the winter they wore robes and capes made from woven plant material. Some were lined with fur. Fur or bird skin caps were also worn in the colder months. In the coldest climates they covered themselves from head to toe with animal furs. In order to sew a hide to fit, they punctured holes in the animal hide with an awl and then fashioned a needle from a bone. They sewed the pieces together using sinew. They would adorn the hides with dentalium shells if they were available. Dentalium shells were a way to show your wealth and were so highly sought after; they traded at a high price. Glass beads were worn by both men and women and were traded amongst the tribes and bands. Wearing the scalps of red-headed woodpeckers was a sign of great wealth for both men and women.

Explorers who visited Southern Oregon wrote in their journals that some of the men were completely naked during the warm months. In other regions, they wore leggings and shirts made of natural materials or hides from animals. During the colder months they covered themselves in animal furs.

When a woman was expecting a baby, she was assisted by midwives who helped with the birth. The baby was splashed with cold water, causing it to gasp for its first breath. The umbilical cord was cut and given to the grandmother. The newborn was rubbed with oil and wrapped in cedar bark cloth before being presented to the relatives. A feast was held to welcome the baby. The grandfather would present a cradle to the new parents. A shaman would place the baby in the new cradle and perform a ceremony. If the baby was a girl, the grandmother would present a root digger that the baby would use her entire life. The father of the newborn would present gifts to the family. The family in turn would give gifts to the baby.

Many parents used a cradleboard to carry their baby for the first year. The cradleboards in Oregon were usually made from cedar. They would hollow out a slim section of a cedar trunk, then line the cradleboard with soft shredded cedar bark. The cedar bark served as both a blanket and a diaper. They made pads of cedar bark to place under the baby's neck. The baby was strapped in with bindings. The parent could carry the baby strapped to their back while they went about their daily chores.

At bath time, the baby would be washed and then covered in fish oil or oil from a whale. The baby would then be covered in willow ash or ochre. In the Rogue Valley, pioneers David and Clarissa Birdseye built a cabin near the Rogue River. When their son James was born, the local Indian woman were so intrigued with a white baby that they would borrow him for the day and take him down to the river. They would play with him and wash him in the river. When they returned the baby, he was always covered in red ochre.

Ceremonies were very important to the Indians. There were ceremonies to honor the first salmon of the season. When a young boy caught his first fish, a ceremony was held. There were seasonal ceremonies for the various roots and plants that marked the changing of the seasons. Ceremonies were held for marriages and births.

The Indians enjoyed gambling and other games. The game of Lahal was a game of chance. Players would use two small objects such as bones that differed in color or statue. Small sticks were placed on a board used for wagering. The object of the game was to conceal the piece of bone in one hand and have the other person guess which hand held the piece of bone. They also played a game known as Shinny. The ball for Shinny was made from two pieces of wood tied six inches apart with buckskin. The Shinny stick was a long pole with a bent end. The goals were branches stuck in the ground. The ball was tossed in the air in the center of the field. The strategy was to move the ball up the field towards the goal without letting the opponent steal the ball. Another game was to roll smooth stones between two sticks that were set upright in the ground. Women played a dice game wherein each die had lines and dots carved on it. They would shake the die in their hands and then throw them on a mat. They won points depending on what showed on each die when it was rolled. The game of hoop and pole was a challenging game that involved making a ring from twigs and attaching cedar bark to it. The ring was rolled on the ground while the players shot arrows at it or threw spears at it.

The Indians revered the land for its natural resources. They depended on it for food and shelter. There were skirmishes between tribes and bands, but nothing could have prepared them for what was to come when the pioneers began arriving in Oregon. The Donation Land Claim Act brought thousands of people across the plains into Oregon. That, along with the gold rush, meant that the land the Indians had known for centuries was about to change forever.

At first things were friendly between the pioneers and the Indians, but as more and more pioneers arrived, things began to change. The pioneers had a different outlook than the Indians when it came to land. They portioned off their plot of land and claimed it as their own. It wasn't long before the Indian's natural resources began to diminish. The new settlers plowed the land, destroying the natural food supply that had grown for centuries. Additionally, their animals grazed on the land and consumed food that the Indians had relied on for generations. The streams and rivers that were usually teaming with fish were now filled with men mining for gold. Once the surface gold had been mined, the miners began doing placer mining. This involved using hydraulic pipes, known as giants, to blast huge amounts of water to bring the gold to the surface. The wide-open land that the Indians relied on for their seeds and berries was now divided into parcels that they could not enter. As more pioneers arrived, the availability of game deceased. The early 1850s saw tremendous storms sweeping through Oregon with heavy snow and flooding. This put an additional strain on their natural resources and food become increasingly scarce. The new settlers brought diseases to Oregon that they were immune to but proved to be deadly to the Indians.

Some of the new settlers saw the plight of the Indians and worked to right some of the wrongs. They would grow extra food in order to give some to the Indians. They shared fish and game with them. John Beeson from the small town of Talent went to Washington, D.C., to fight for the rights of the Indians. In a letter written from Camp Warner on November 9, 1867, Julie S. Gilliss wrote, in part:

> The persecution of the Indians goes against the grain with me. I think it is a wretched unholy warfare; the poor creatures are hunted down like wild beasts and shot down in cold blood. The same ball went through a mother and her baby at her breast. One poor little creature just the size of my baby was shot because he would someday grow up.

Tensions ran high between the new settlers and the Indians. It wasn't long before small skirmishes broke out. These in turn became outright wars. From time-to-time, peace treaties were signed that had varying levels of long-term success. But by the mid-1850s, the Rogue River Indian Wars took over a large portion of Southern Oregon. The U.S. government concluded that the situation was becoming increasingly dangerous for both sides. The U.S. government appointed Joel Palmer as the superintendent of Indian Affairs. When things still did not improve, President Pierce issued an executive order for the relocation of all Indians living in Southern Oregon. In 1855, Agent Palmer organized the Oregon Mounted Volunteers and the U.S. Army to round up all of the Indians in Southern Oregon. They led the Indians to the Siletz Reservation and the Grand Ronde Reservation. The government constructed forts at each reservation and stationed officers at each post to ensure that no one left the reservations.

The Siletz Reservation was heavily forested when the Indians arrived. They worked clearing some of the land so that crops could be planted. They created three groups of farms, known as the Lower, Middle and Upper Farms. The government provided horses, wagons, plows, mowing machines, harvesters, and threshing machines. They grew vegetables, oats, barley, wheat, and hay for their own consumption and sold the excess for profit. The government set up a blacksmith shop, a sawmill, and a planer. The Indians raised cattle, horses, sheep, pigs, cows, and poultry. They sold butter, eggs, and milk. The government set up schools for the children and vocational schools for the adults. There were two stores and a post office. Additionally, there was a medical doctor, a judge, and police officers. The Indians who lived on the Siletz Reservation became self-sufficient within the first decade. In addition to farming and raising stock, they cut timber and sold it to local mills. Woman made extra baskets and sold them. Some of the Indians found day jobs on local farms picking berries, hops, and fruit. Others worked in the fishing industry.

In 1866, the Indians were relocated to one area of the Siletz Reservation. In 1891, the government gave every man, woman, and child eighty acres of land on the Siletz Reservation. However, there were stipulations such as they could not sell the land, only lease it. On May 21, 1895, the rest of the land on the Siletz Reservation was declared "open to settlement" meaning that anyone could buy parcels of land.

An estimated 3,000 Indians were sent to live on the Siletz Reservation. The 1905 census showed 416 Indians remaining. Diseases had taken the lives of many, others died in conflict amongst the tribes and bands, and natural causes claimed others.

Approximately 4,000 Indians were sent to the Grand Ronde Reservation. This reservation was similar to the Siletz in that the Indians established farms and began working the land. A sawmill was constructed along with a blacksmith shop. A store was built to serve the residents. There was a medical doctor on site, along with a judge and small police force. In 1856, Agent Palmer wrote a letter to his supervisor, George Manypenny, the Commissioner of Indian Affairs in Washington, D.C. In the letter he described the reservation:

> Active operations are going forward upon the reservation. Considerable progress is being made in putting in wheat crops, rendered more necessary by that sown in the fall having, with nearly the entire fields in the country, been killed by the severity of the frost in early January. Small tracts of land are being designated and marked off for residence and cultivation by the

respective members of the bands, and with but few exceptions, they appear to enter into the arrangement with spirit and determination to do something for themselves.

Although there was a day school and a boarding school, many parents were hesitant to send their children to either school. The schools taught English in an attempt to suppress the children's native languages. The children were encouraged to live in a dormitory. The schools taught the basics with an emphasis on vocational agriculture. There was much distrust between the parents and the schools. The parents feared that the children would lose their native traditions.

In the beginning, the Grand Ronde Reservation was not conductive to growing crops due to the poor soil and the climate. The Indians did not have the skills needed to raise stock or operate heavy equipment. The grist mill that the government provided, was continually under repair. It took many years to prime the soil and learn how to grow crops, raise stock, and operate heavy machinery. Despite a rough start, by the early 1870s, the Indians were entirely self-sufficient and were no longer receiving any subsidies from the government.

In the early 1860s, the Indians were allowed to obtain day passes that allowed them to leave the reservation during the day to work in the nearby areas. Some of the men and women found work as field laborers on the nearby farms. Women also worked in private homes doing housework, and they sold their handmade baskets to earn money. Men were allowed to leave the reservation to fish on the Salmon River to supplement the food supply on the reservation and to sell the fish to locals.

The government eventually gave the head of each family living on the Grand Ronde reservation 160 acres, allotted in three land parcels; one for grazing, one that was suitable for growing crops, and one parcel that had timber. Children were given forty acres and adults were allotted eighty acres. By the early 1890s, only about 350 Indians remained at the Grand Ronde reservation. Many of the Indians had succumbed to diseases and death.

In 1904, the U.S. government began the process of selling two million acres of land on reservations. The acreage that was part of the Grand Ronde Reservation totaled 26,300 acres. The government advertised that the lands "embrace valuable agriculture and timber tracts, and may be had by those who desire to secure them for a small fraction of their real value." The minimum bid was $1 per acre with a minimum of 100 acres per buyer.

The relocation of the Indians to the Siletz Reservation and the Grand Ronde Reservation were not the only relocations that occurred in Oregon. The earliest conflict was the Cayuse War. It began with the Whitman Massacre in 1847. In the beginning the Cayuse Indians were on good terms with the Whitman missionaries who assured them they were there to help. It wasn't long though before the Indians saw their natural resources diminishing as more and more people came to the mission. After a measles epidemic killed many of their tribe, the Indians murdered fourteen of the missionaries including Marcus and Narcissa Whitman. The Indians did not understand the measles disease. They believed the missionaries were poisoning them and ruining their land. The U.S. government sent in troops, but it became apparent that the war would not end quickly. The war dragged on for seven years before the Cayuse Indians were sent to live on a reservation. The Yakima War, the Bannock War, the Modoc War, and the Nez Pierce War all ended with the Indians being sent to live on reservations throughout Oregon. A few of the other reservation the Indians were sent to include Klamath Reservation, Malheur and Burns Reservation, Warm Springs Reservation, and Umatilla Reservation. Each of the reservations held members of varying tribes and bands, most of whom did not speak the same language.

At the end of life, most of the Indians were buried, although there were some cremations. In some areas, the deceased were placed in a wooden box and buried in their canoe along with their possessions. Others were laid to rest underground with their prized possessions. One group of early explorers wrote, "a number of Indian graves, they were surrounded with poles, one end of which was stuck in the ground, to the others were suspended the goods of the deceased, such as mats, blankets, bows, and arrows." After observing a Takelma Indian burial in Josephine County, explorer Peter Ogden wrote, "Amongst the different Indian tribes that I have seen, those in this quarter are the first who come as near to our mode of inter[r]ing their dead. The graves are sunk from five to six feet deep, the body carefully wrapt in deer skins and at the head and feet, square planks are erected. The head as is almost invariable the plan with all Indians, placed towards the East."

What no one could have foretold during this time of conflict was that more than a century later, archaeological excavations would be done to learn more about the Indians who lived in Southern Oregon, and throughout the United States. Fragments of baskets and mats were located at many of the excavation sites. The materials used for the baskets and mats included twisted tule, hazel and willow twigs, pine root, and juncus. Animal bones as well as fish bones were common finds. The bones varied in species depending on the area of Southern Oregon. Various tools were uncovered to include projectile points, unifacially flaked tools, scrapers, drills, gravers, knives, cores, and choppers. The projectile points differed in shape and the material used depending on the region. Other items unearthed included pestles, mortars, mullers, milling stones, basalt bowls, hammer stones, net sinkers, steatite ornaments, beads, and occasionally shells. Parts of bows, sinew, and rope snares were uncovered. Bits of bulbs, berries, and seeds showed some of the local food sources.

1

Malheur and Harney Counties

Harney County was created in 1889 and is the largest county in Oregon. The county, as well as Harney Valley and Harney Lake, were named for William Selby Harney. He was the Brigadier-General for the Department of Oregon, U.S. Army in 1858. He is credited for seizing the San Juan Islands from the British in 1859. He served in the Black Hawk War, the Mexican War, and the Civil War.

Malheur County was taken from Baker County in 1887. It is the second largest county in Oregon. In 1931, the name was almost changed to Sinnott County to honor Nicholas Sinnott, a state representative, who had recently died. The bill passed the House, but not the Senate.

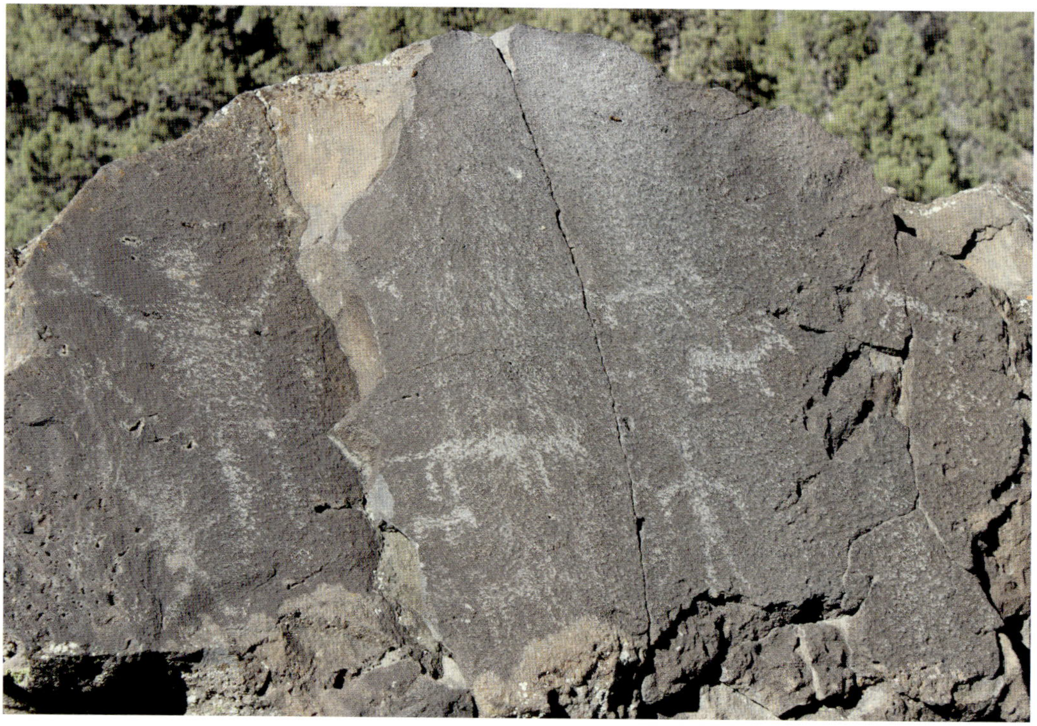

Malheur County has a very interesting history including many ancient petroglyphs.

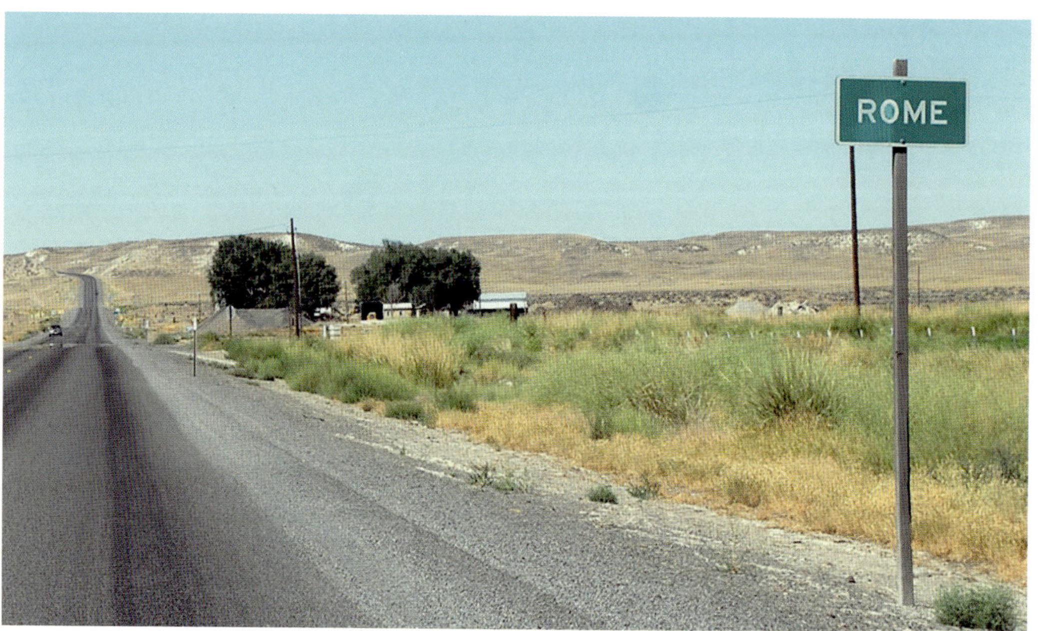

Rome, Oregon, got its start in 1909 when the town was established. It was named after the unique rock formations.

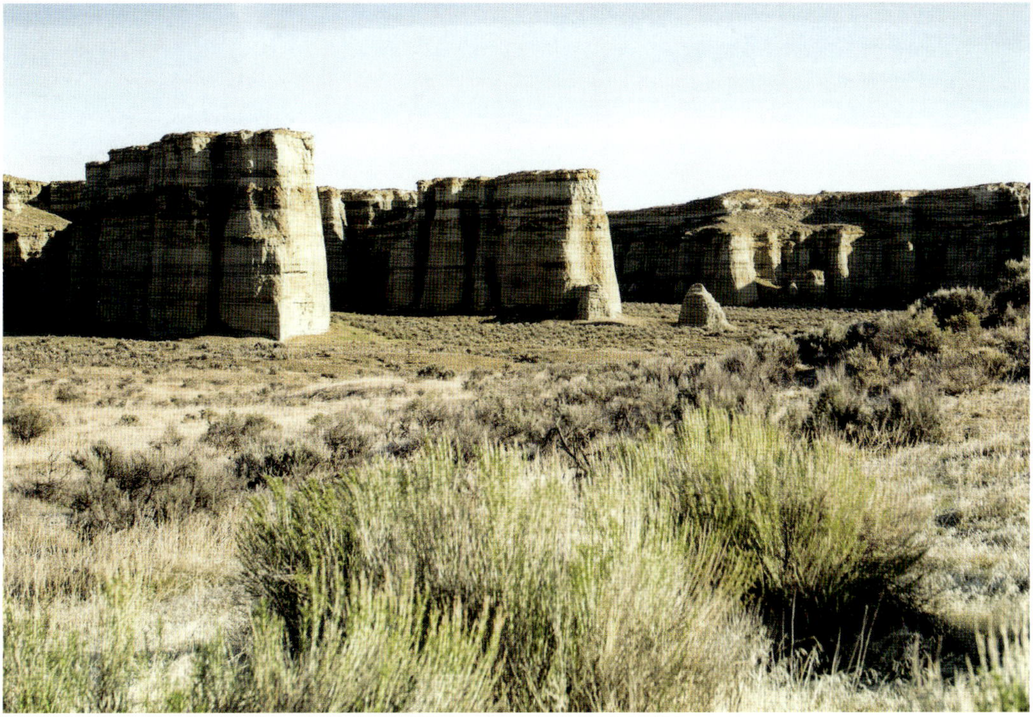

Rome, Oregon. was not built in a day.

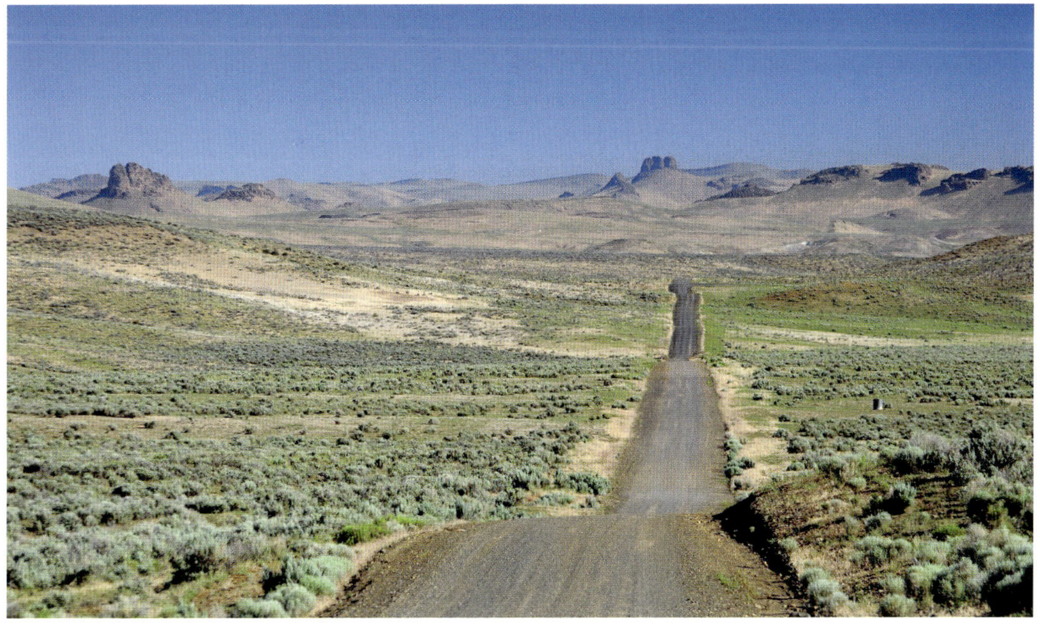

This long road leads to Leslie Gulch and Three Fingers Rock.

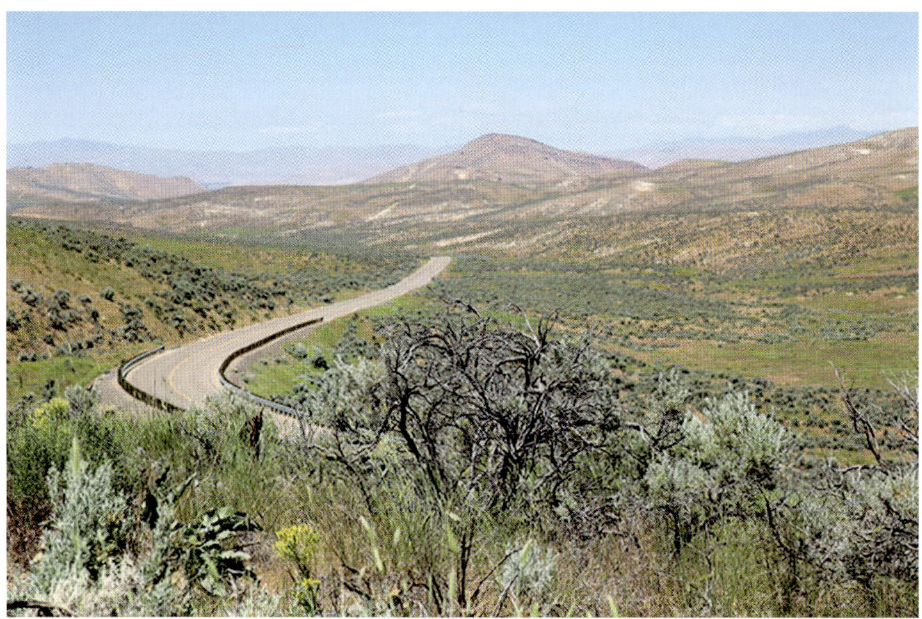

Kenney Pass in Vale shows the actual ruts in the ground where covered wagons passed through in the 1800s. Vale was the very first stop in Oregon for the pioneers. Originally there was just a trading post but over time that trading post grew into an actual town that was named Vale. Kenney Pass is named for Johnathan Keeney who offered weary travelers a place to stay in his cabin and barn.

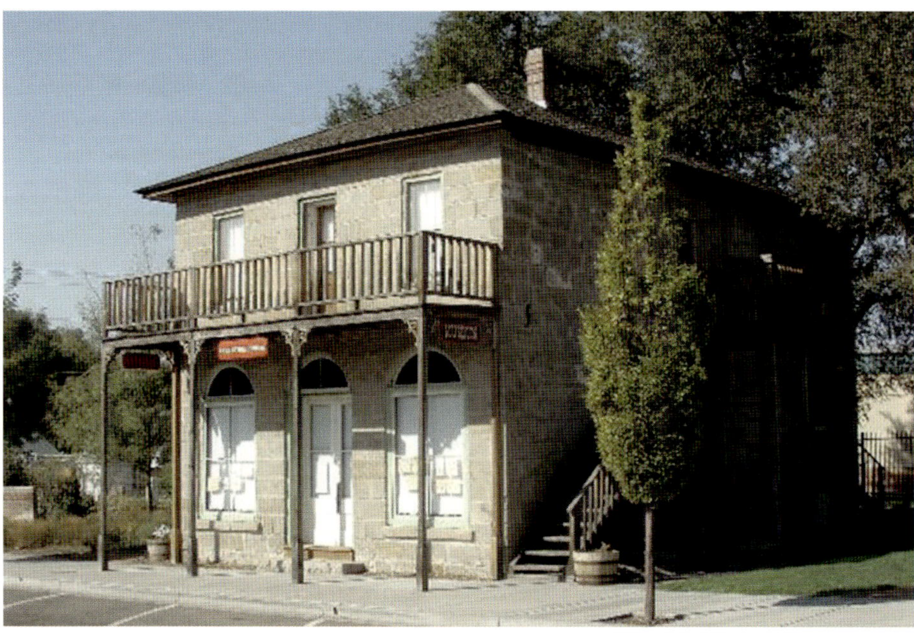

Johnathan Keeney's cabin was replaced by the Rinehart House in 1872.

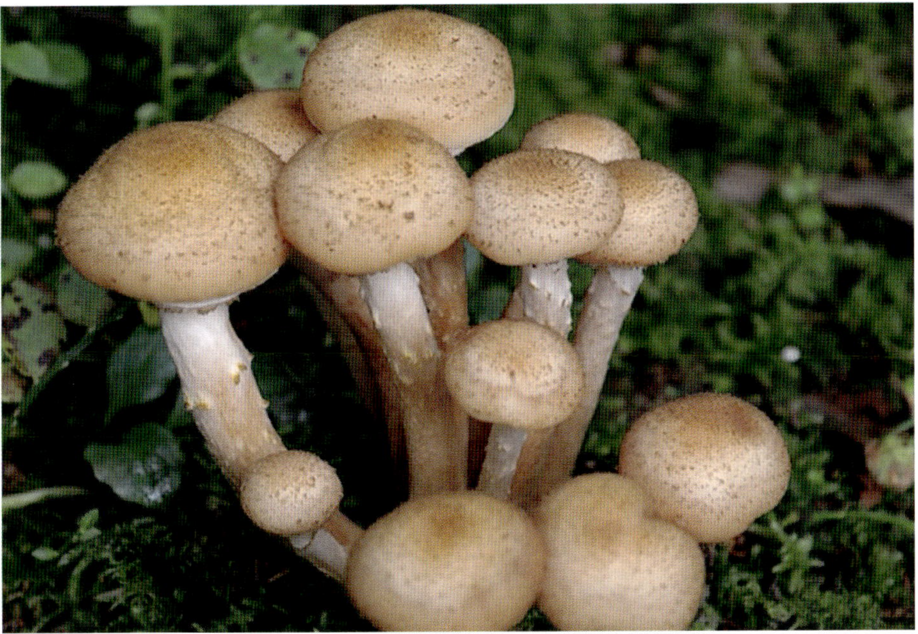

Malheur County is famous for their Humongous Fungus, or the Honey Mushroom. It is thought to be the largest living organism in the world based on mass, area, and volume. It is estimated to be at least 8,000 years old. It covers approximately 2,240 acres and weighs an estimated 35,000 tons.

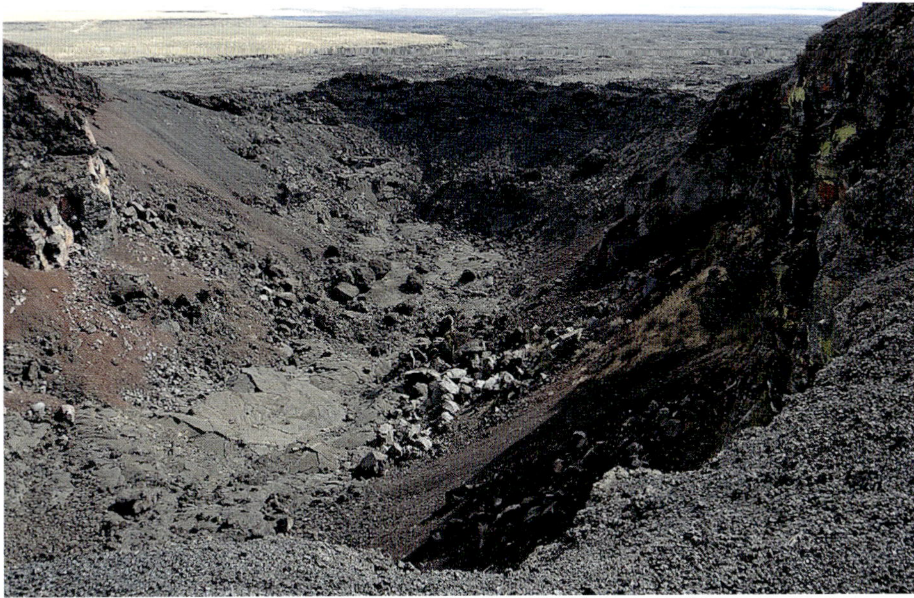

Jordan Crater covers an area that is twenty-seven square miles. The depth is 150 feet. Although it is thought to be the youngest of all lava flows that have occurred in Oregon, it is thousands of years old.

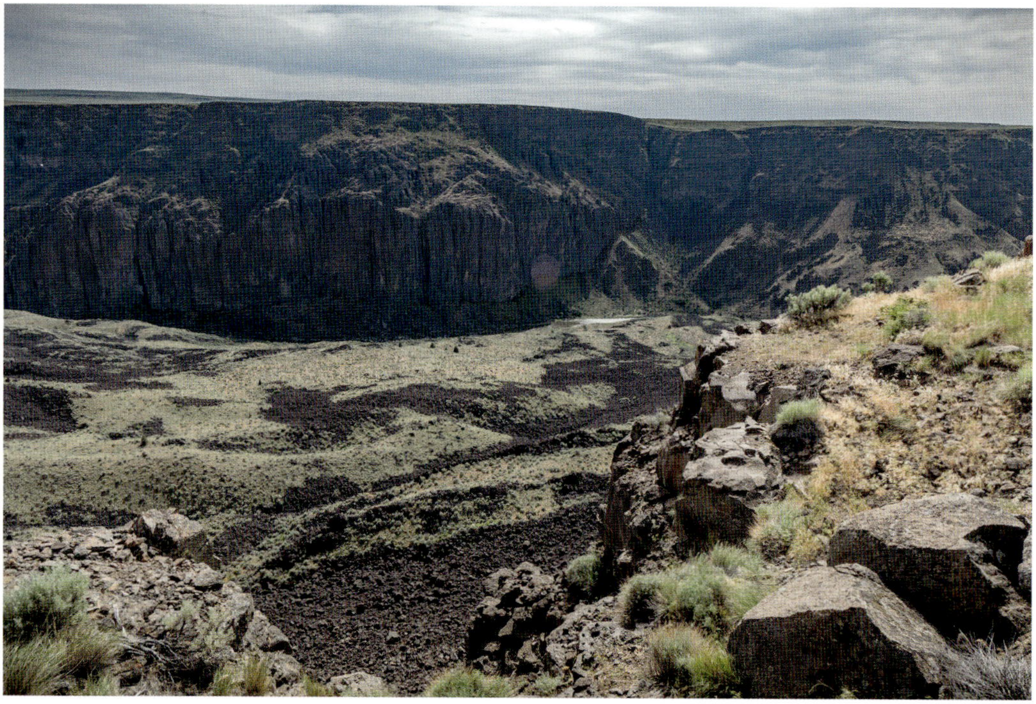

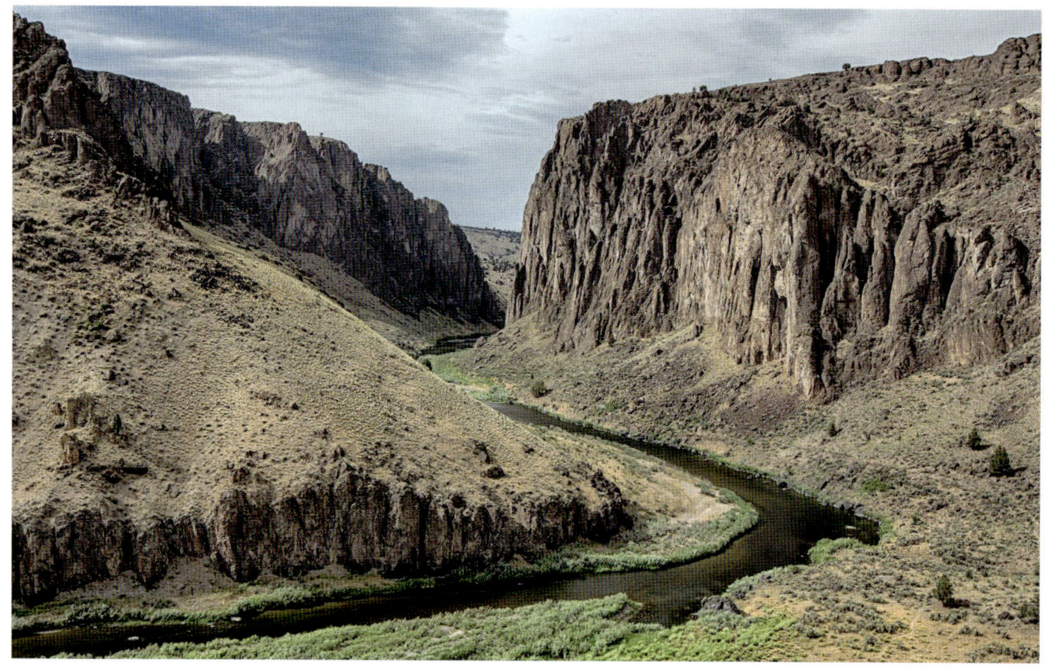

The Owyhee Canyonlands stretches through three states: Oregon, Idaho, and Nevada.

The Owyhee, Bruneau, and Jarbidge rivers run through the Owyhee Canyon.

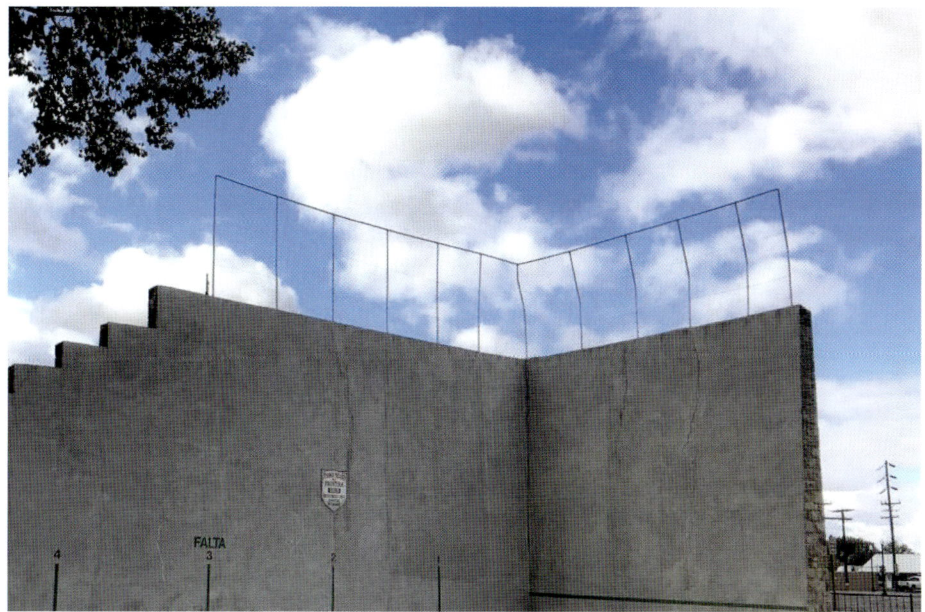

The handball court pictured is called a pelota fronton. It was built in Jordan Valley in 1915 by Basque nationals. At the time two-thirds of the population in Jordan Valley were Basque nationals. They worked as sheepherders, a skill they had acquired in their homeland. The walls of the court were built from stones they carried from a quarry outside of Jordan Valley. They covered the interior walls with an earthen mortar.

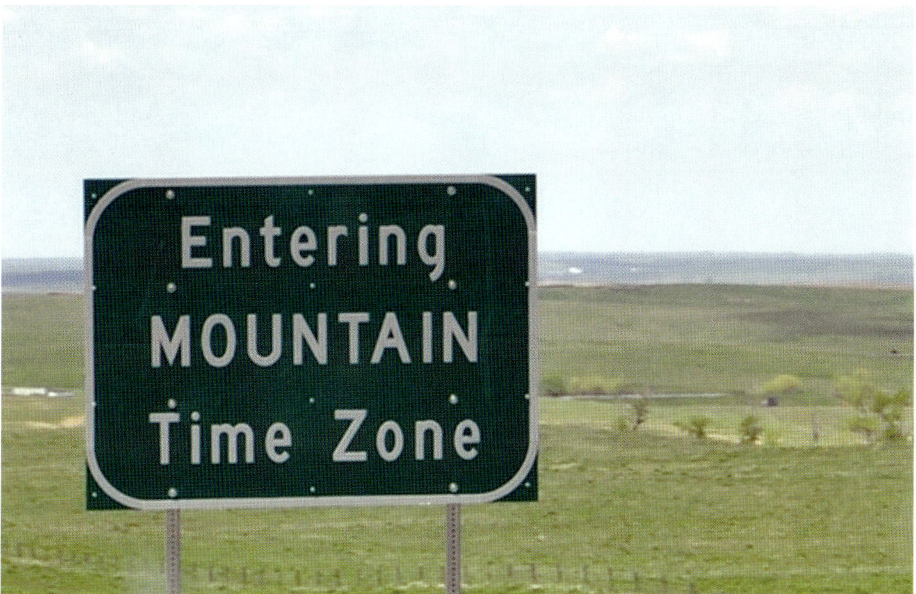

Parts of Malheur County is in the Mountain Time Zone. Whereas the rest of the county, along with the rest of Oregon, is in the Pacific Time Zone.

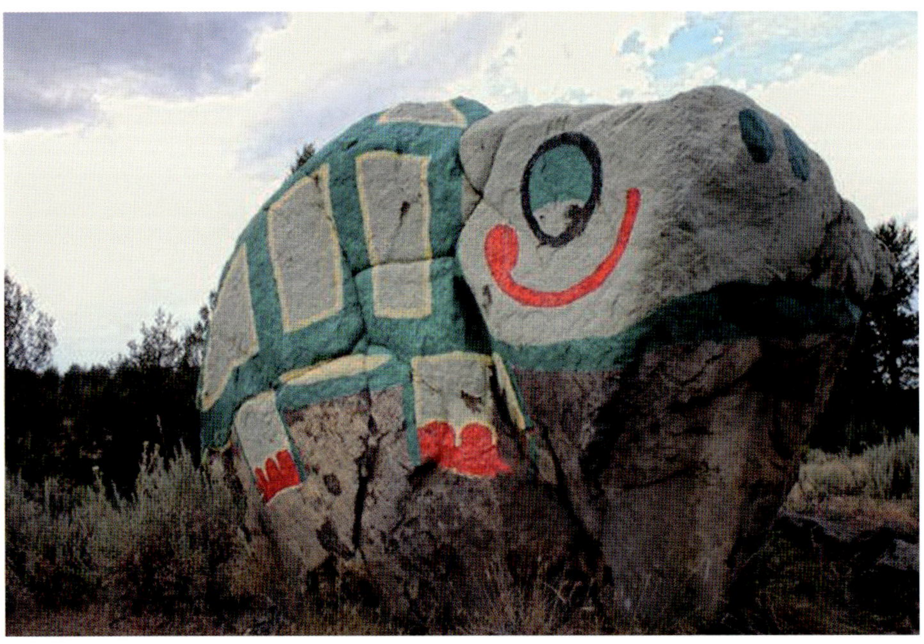

This painted rock, located on Pine Creek Road, was made to look like a turtle. It is fifteen feet tall.

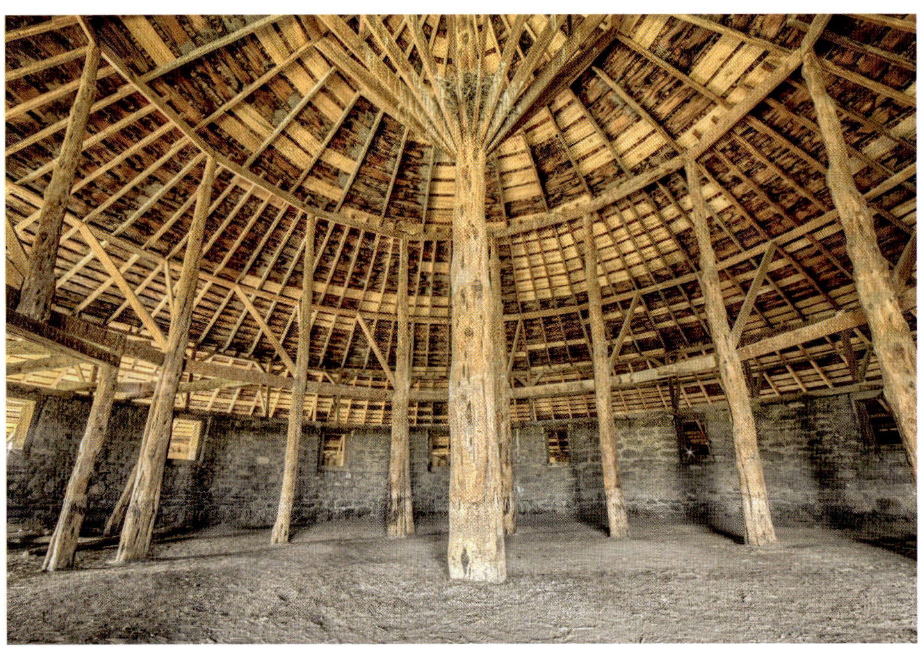

Peter French arrived in Harney County in 1872 and began acquiring land and cattle. He constructed this round barn out of ponderosa pine. The barn measures approximately 100 feet in diameter. There are twenty-nine peeled juniper poles supporting the structure. Inside the barn is a circular stone wall that is nine feet tall and eighteen inches thick. The center post pictured is twenty-five feet tall.

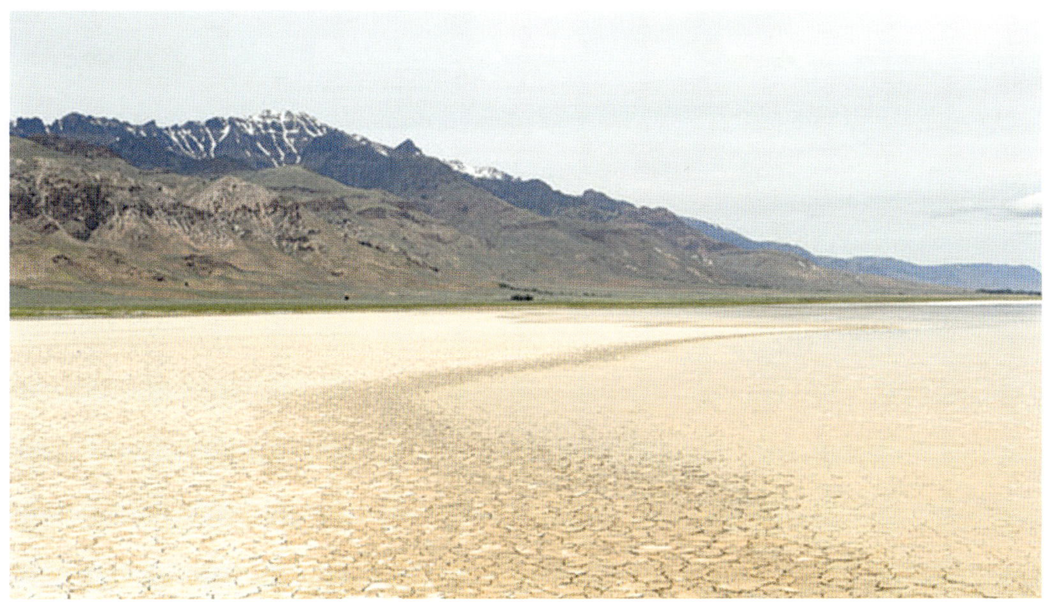

Thousands of years ago, Lake Alvord covered all of what is now known as Alvord Desert. Today the Alvord Playa Lake only receives a few inches of rain a year. The rain can only escape through evaporation. When that happens, precipitated salt minerals are left behind.

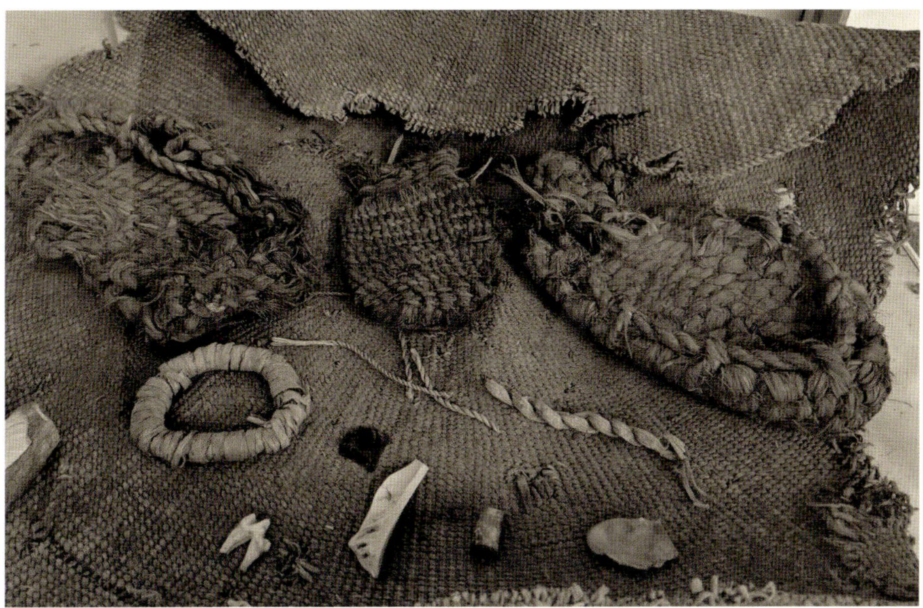

When David Stine arrived in Harney County in 1874, he discovered a beautiful area that he named for his employer, John Catlow. He described the area as a cattleman's paradise. Many years later archeologists uncovered the unique items pictured in the Catlow Valley during an excavation. The materials and weaving techniques indicate that the items could be at least 8,000 years old. Other items excavated include stone tools, fragments of leather, and remnants of rock pits.

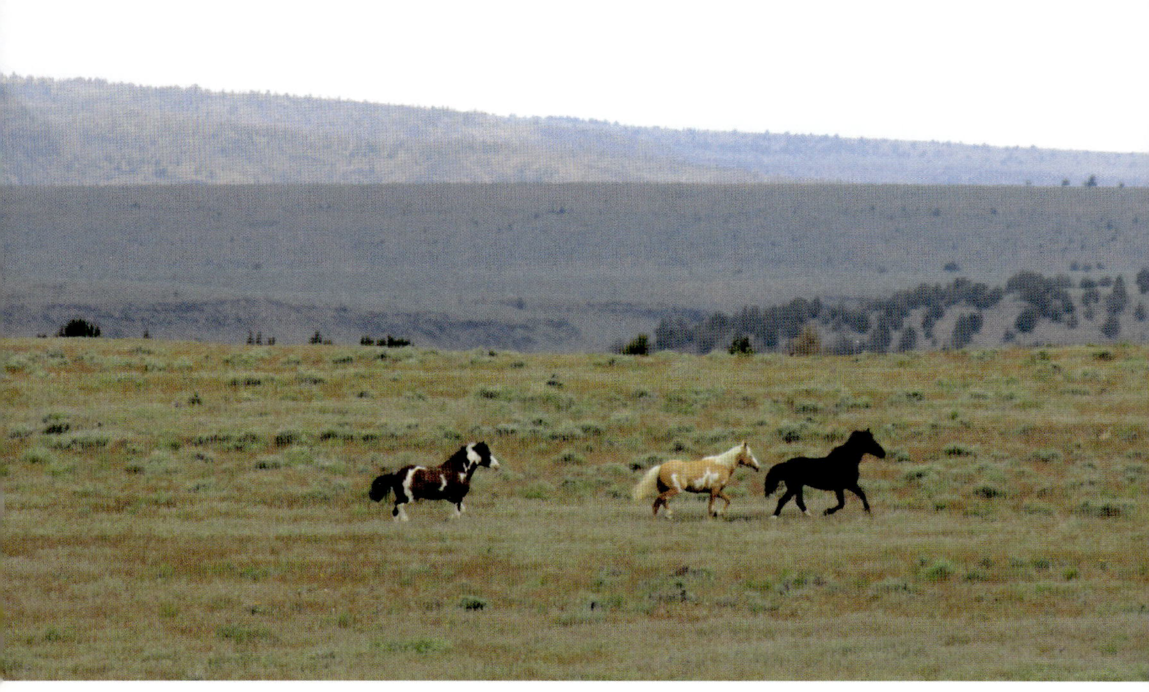

The Donner and Blitzen River was not named for Santa's reindeer, but instead for the German words for thunder and lightning. The river was named by German immigrants who were caught in a thunder and lightning storm while trying to cross the river.

Opposite page: It was not long after Pearl Harbor was bombed that the Exclusion Act was signed into law. All people of Japanese ancestry were ordered to report to internment camps. One of those camps was in Tule Lake, just over the Oregon-California border. Eventually some of the prisoners were sent to camps in Harney and Malheur counties. They worked as field laborers, building railroads, and in factories.

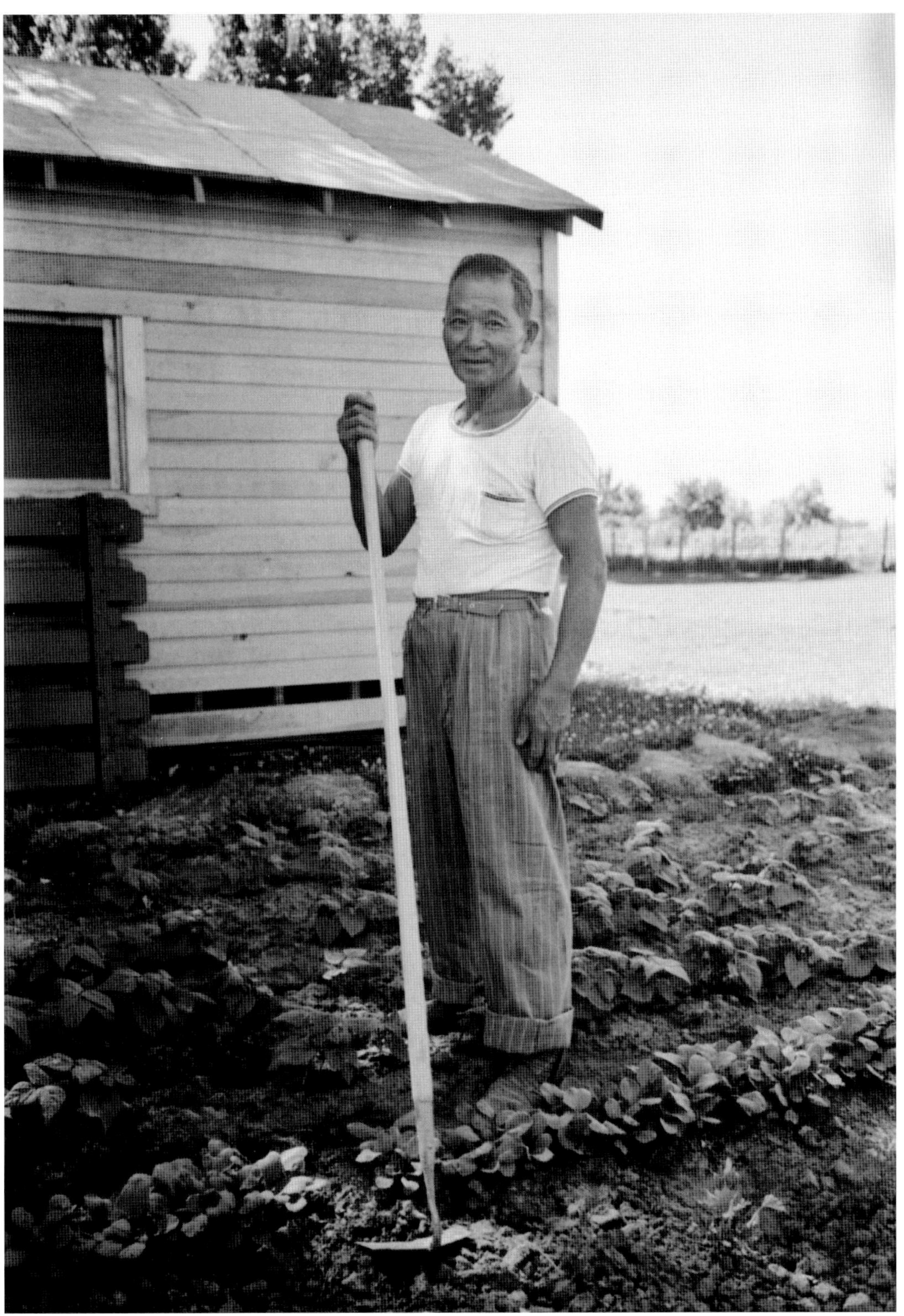

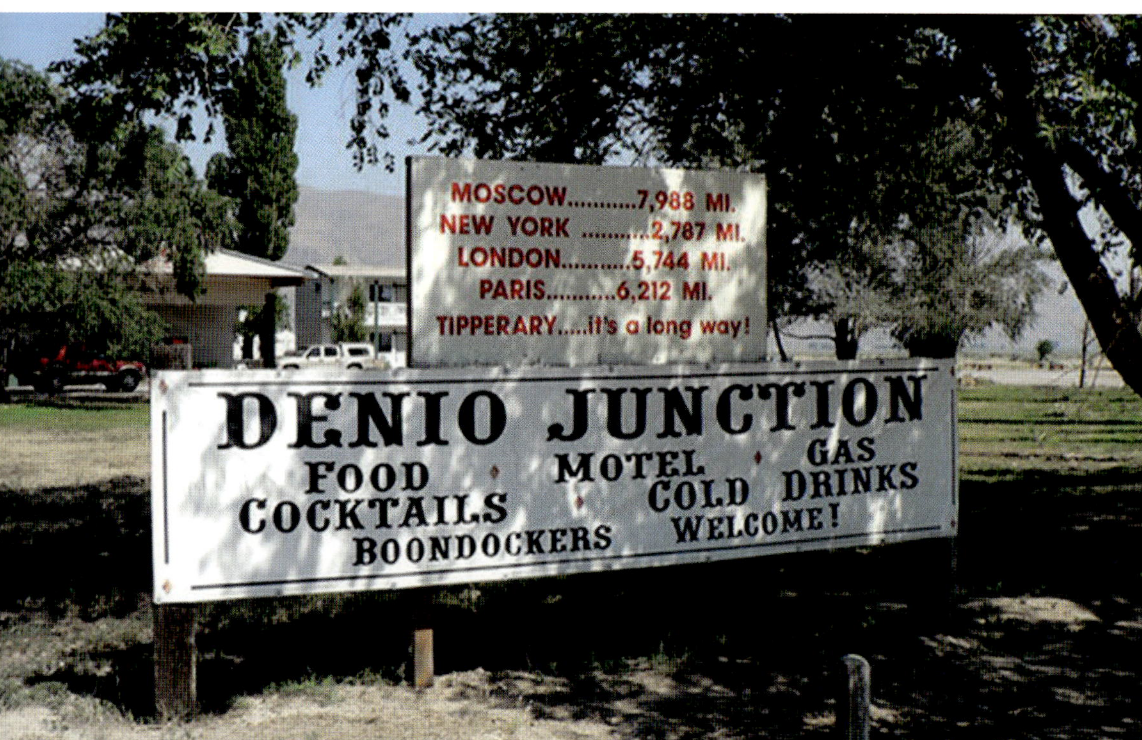

The town of Denio has the unique designation of being in both Oregon and Nevada, straddling the border. The town was named for Aaron Denio, who came overland in 1860. In 1888 he established a post office filing documents as Denio, Oregon. Decades ago, the townsfolk picked up the post office and moved it into Nevada.

2

LAKE AND KLAMATH COUNTIES

Explorer Peter Skeen Ogden referred to "Claminitt Country" in his journal dated July 1, 1826. That same year, explorer David Douglas wrote in his journal about "Clamite." Klamath County was established in 1862, when the government split off a portion of Lake County.

Lake County was named for the abundance of lakes in their region. The county was taken from parts of Jackson County and Wasco County in 1874.

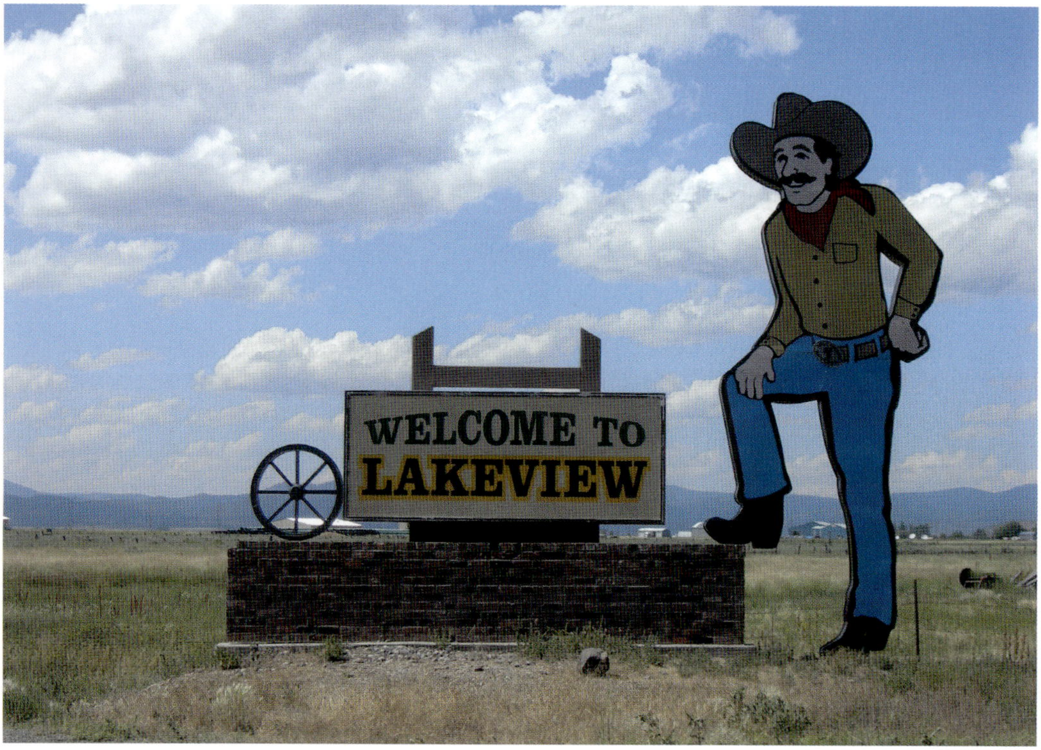

The town of Lakeview is the tallest town in Oregon. The elevation of Lakeview is 4,802 feet above sea level.

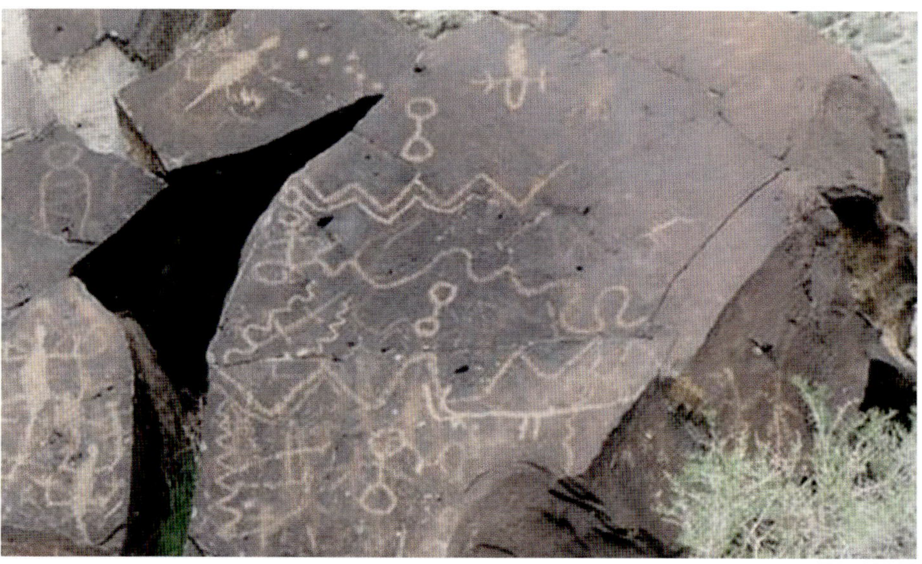

Known as the Greaser Petroglyph, this ancient carving is located near Adel. It is thought to be at least 7,500 years old. It has been on the National Register of Historic Places since 1974.

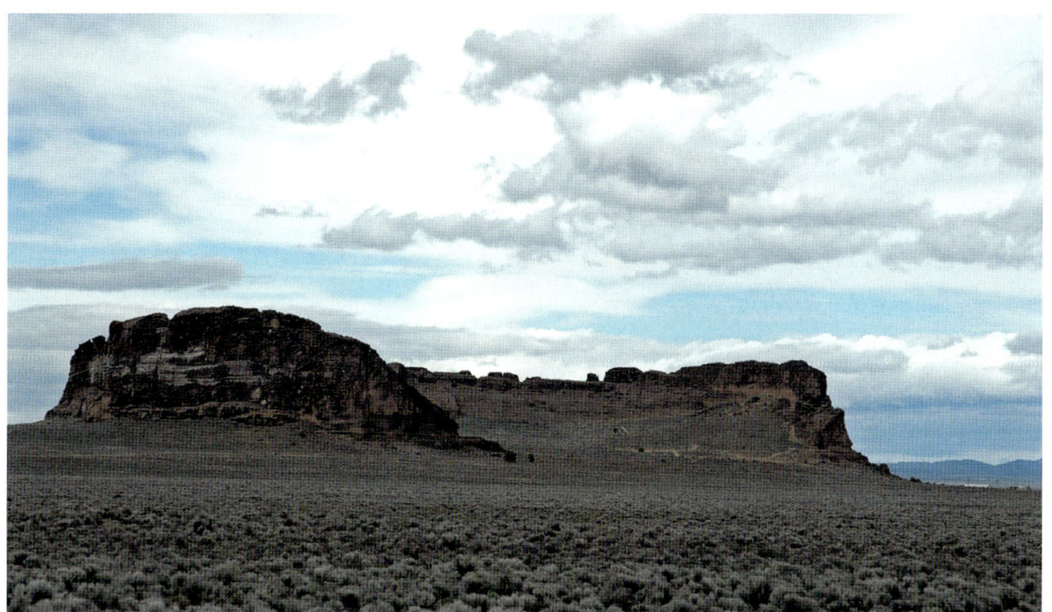

Fort Rock is a tuff ring located on an Ice Age lake bed. It was originally an island. It measures approximately 4,460 feet in diameter and stands an estimated 200 feet tall. Fort Rock was created when basalt magma rose to the surface and encountered the lake bottom.

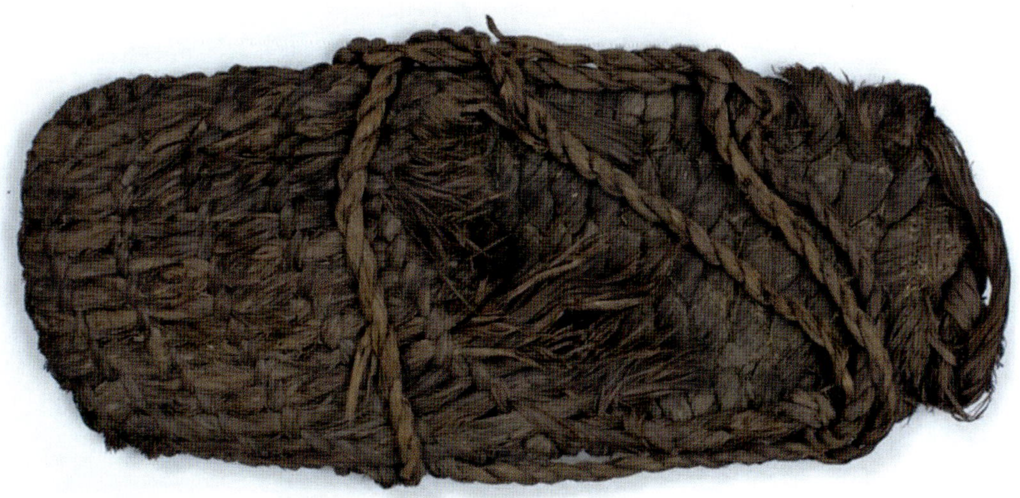

These woven sagebrush sandals were located in Fort Rock Cave. They are estimated to be more than 9,000 years old based on radiocarbon dating. The sandals are thought to be the oldest known footwear in the world. These sandals and others similar to them were located underneath volcanic ash that was determined to be from the eruption of Mount Mazama which occurred an estimated 7,700 years ago.

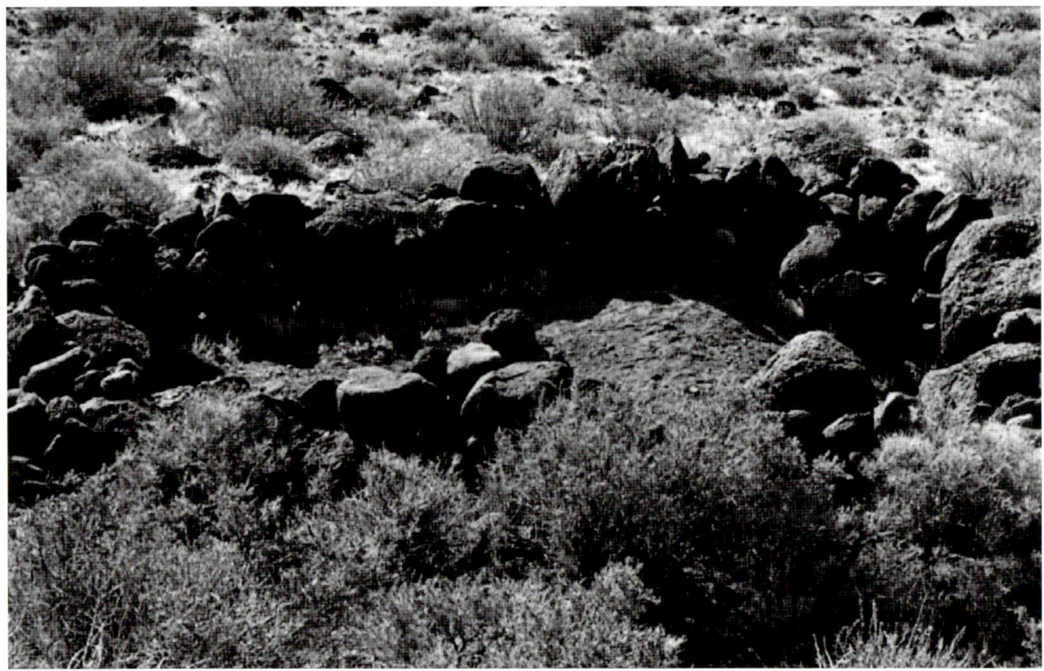

These ancient rock formations are in the East Lake Abert Archeological District in Lake County. The district includes stone house rings such as the one pictured as well as ancient petroglyphs.

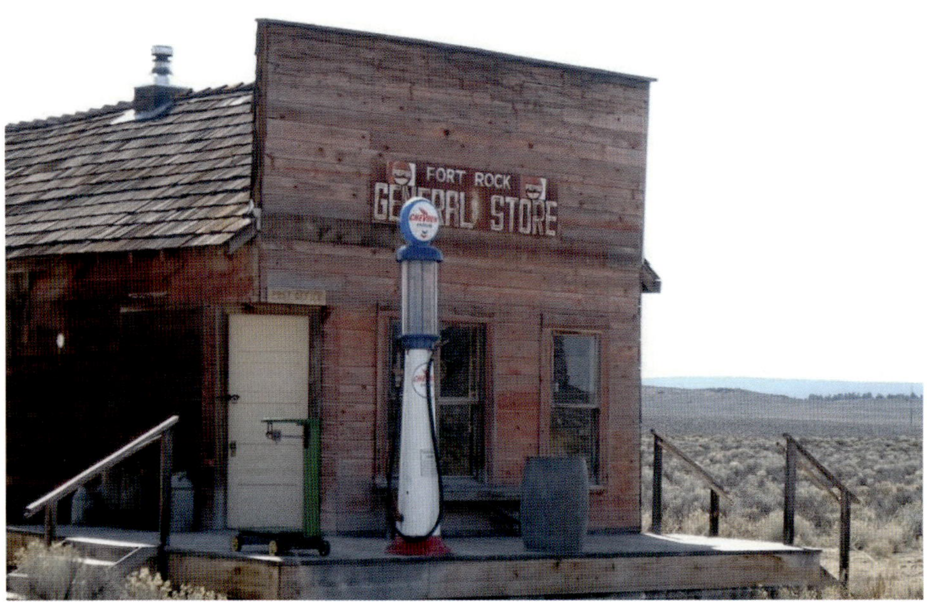

It has been a long time since a customer walked through the doors of the Fort Rock General Store. It has since been preserved and is part of the Homestead Village Museum in Lake County.

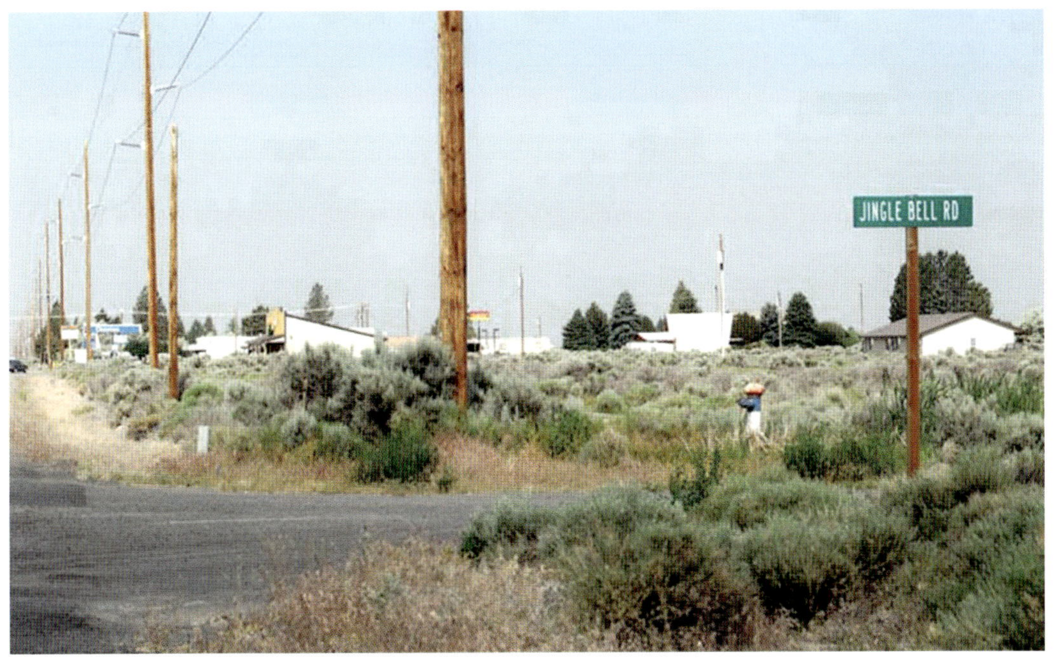

A drive through Christmas Valley shows street signs such as Jingle Bell Road. In the early 1960s, developers tried to market Christmas Valley as the answer to overcrowded cities.

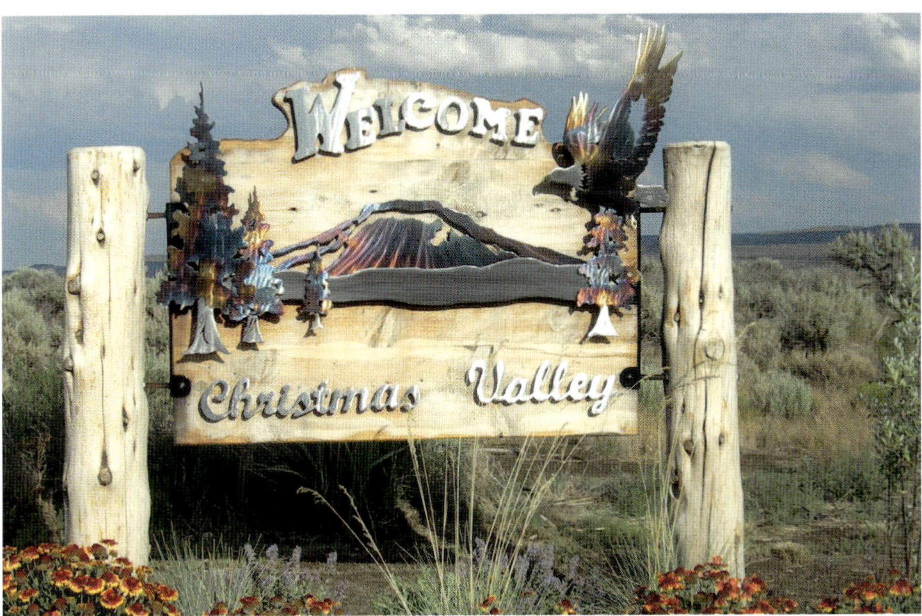

The developers of Christmas Valley built a lodge, three model homes, an artificial lake, an eight-unit motel, and an air field. Their company planes brought people from southern California trying to entice them to buy plots of land starting at $59 an acre. In the end, it was not a successful project.

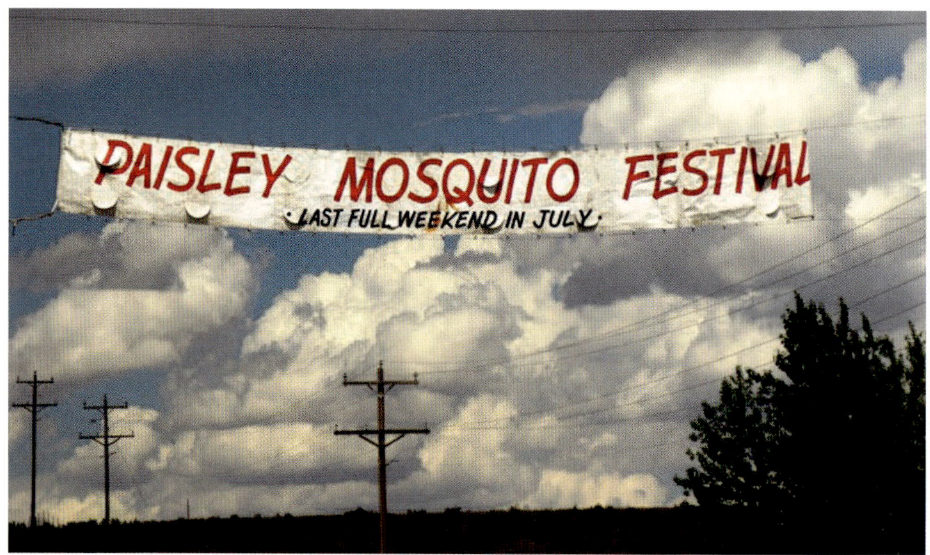

The town of Paisley celebrates the one insect most people find bothersome.

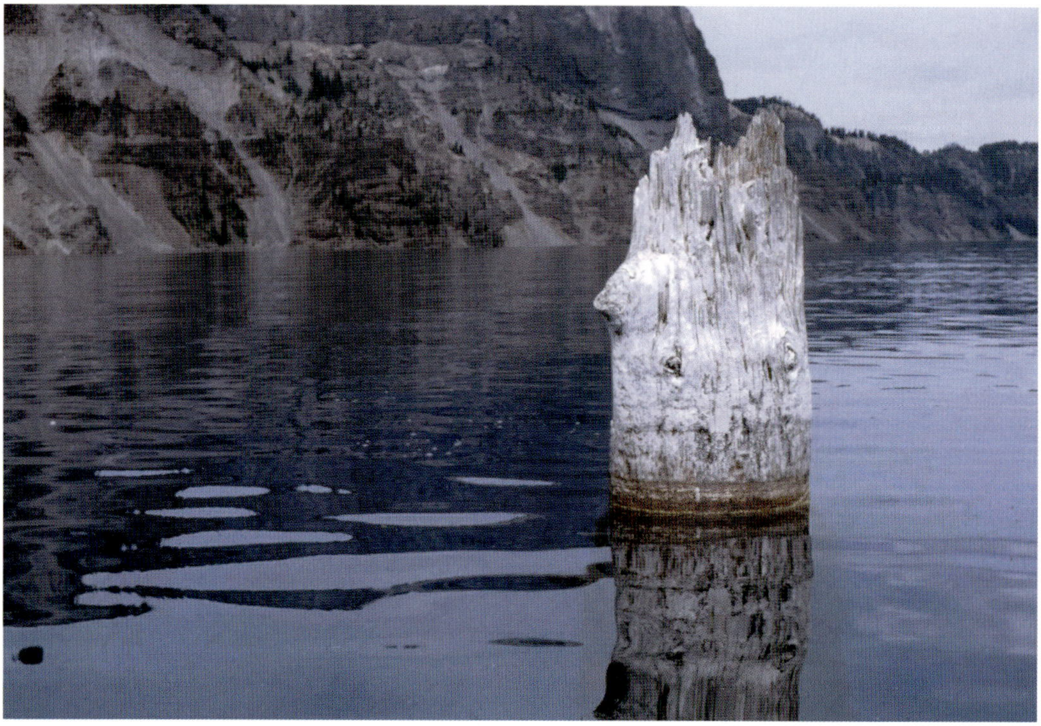

Known as the "Old Man of the Lake," this log has been floating vertically in Crater Lake for at least 125 years. It is thought to be a hemlock tree. The diameter measures approximately two feet and it rises about four feet above the water. The Old Man travels a great distance around the lake. [*Photo courtesy of Crater Lake National Park*]

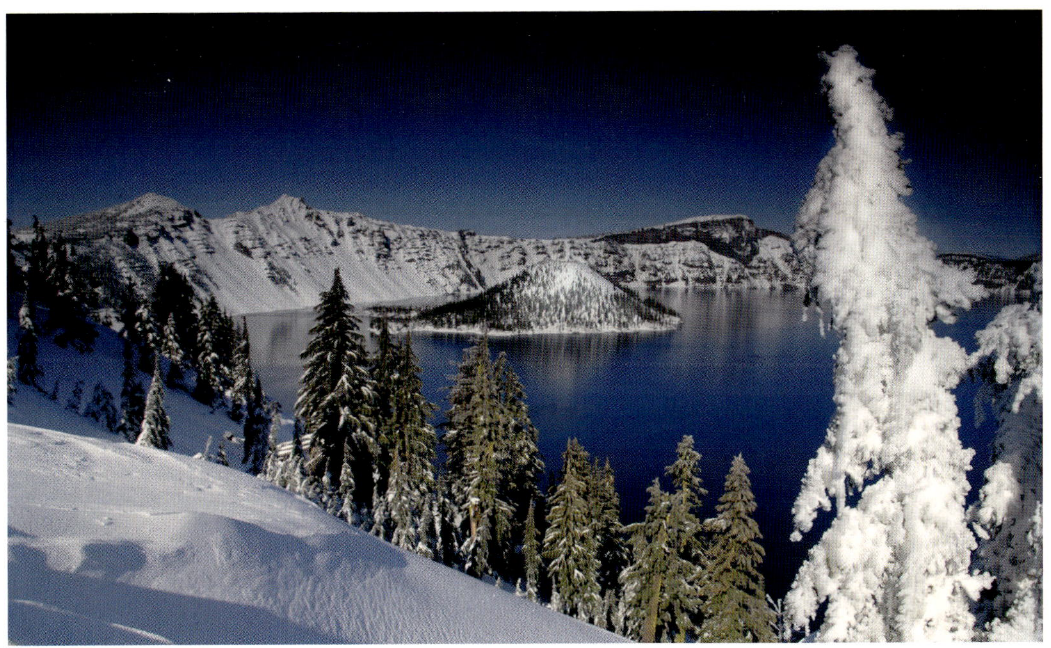

One of the volcanoes along the Cascade Range was Mount Mazama. For more than a half-million years, Mount Mazama had small eruptions that spewed pumice, ash, and cinders. Over time, magna vents and cones developed on the mass of this volcano, which weakened its structure. Approximately 7,700 years ago, the volcano had such a massive eruption that it could no longer support itself, and it collapsed, leaving a huge caldera.

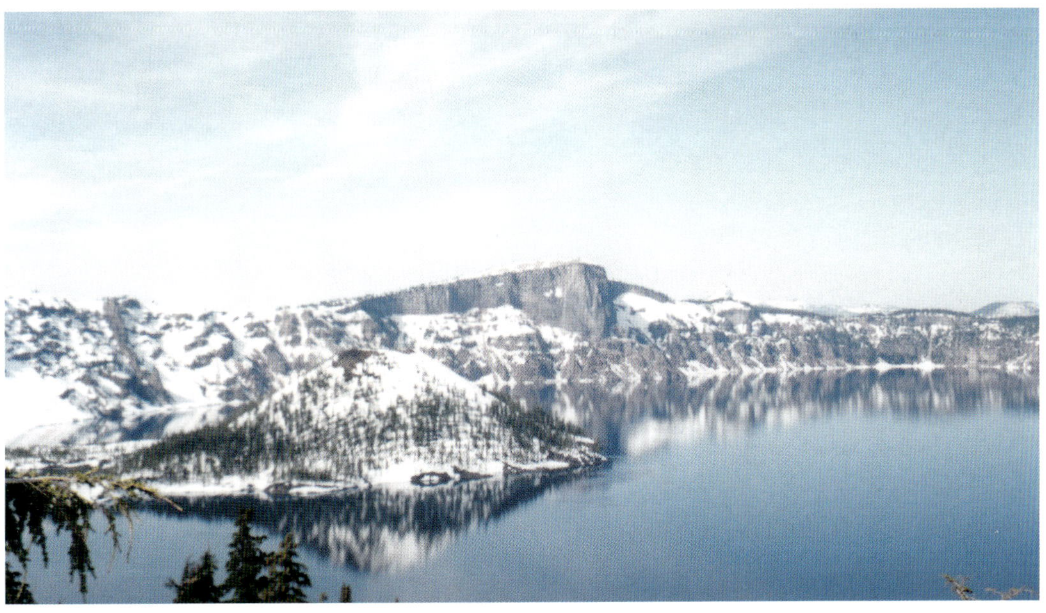

Over time there were additional rumblings, which is how Wizard Island and the Merriam cones came into existence. They are considered volcanoes within a volcano.

At first, the surface of the caldera was too hot to hold water, but eventually the volcanic action subsided. Over the past centuries, the caldera filled with rain and melted snow. Today that caldera is known as Crater Lake. It is the deepest lake in the United States with a maximum depth of 1,943 feet. The depth of the lake remains fairly stable between evaporation and new precipitation.

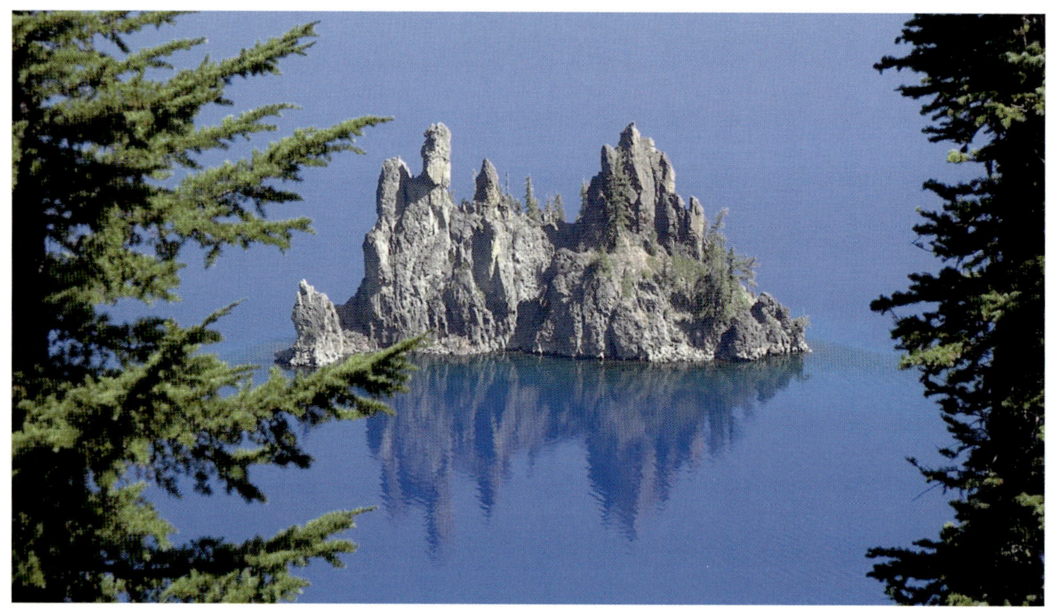

Captain Sprague was part of Company I of the First Oregon Volunteer Infantry out of nearby Fort Klamath. Upon seeing the lake for the first time in 1865, he named this mass "phantom ship" due to its resemblance to a ship. It is said to be a "phantom ship" due to the fact that it can disappear from the scenery and not be seen again for a time.

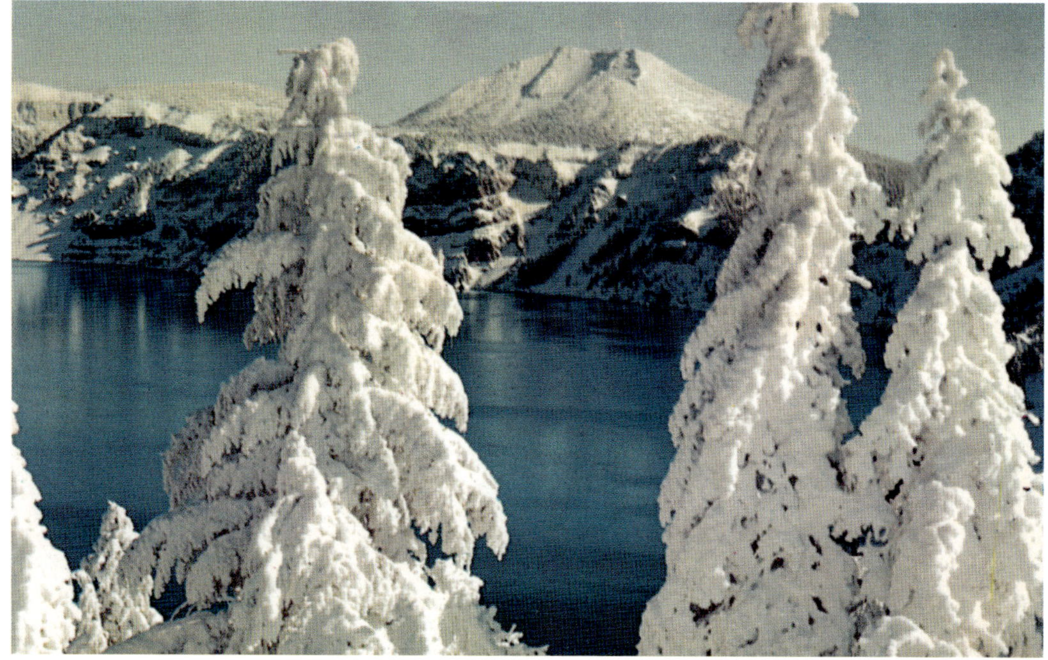

Crater Lake is known for its snowfall. During the winter of 1931-1932, Crater Lake received sixty-five feet of snow at Government Camp and eighty-five to ninety feet at the rim.

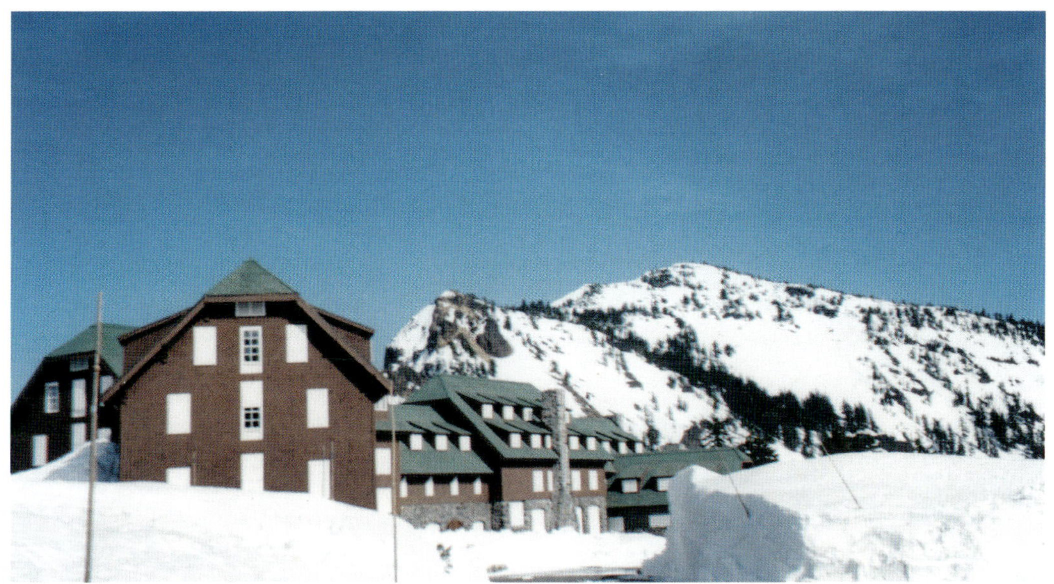

In 1909, construction began on the lodge. Numerous challenges presented themselves, not the least of which was attempting to accommodate a three-month building season and hauling all the construction materials by horse-drawn wagons at an elevation of 6,000 feet. Despite the many difficulties, construction was completed in 1915.

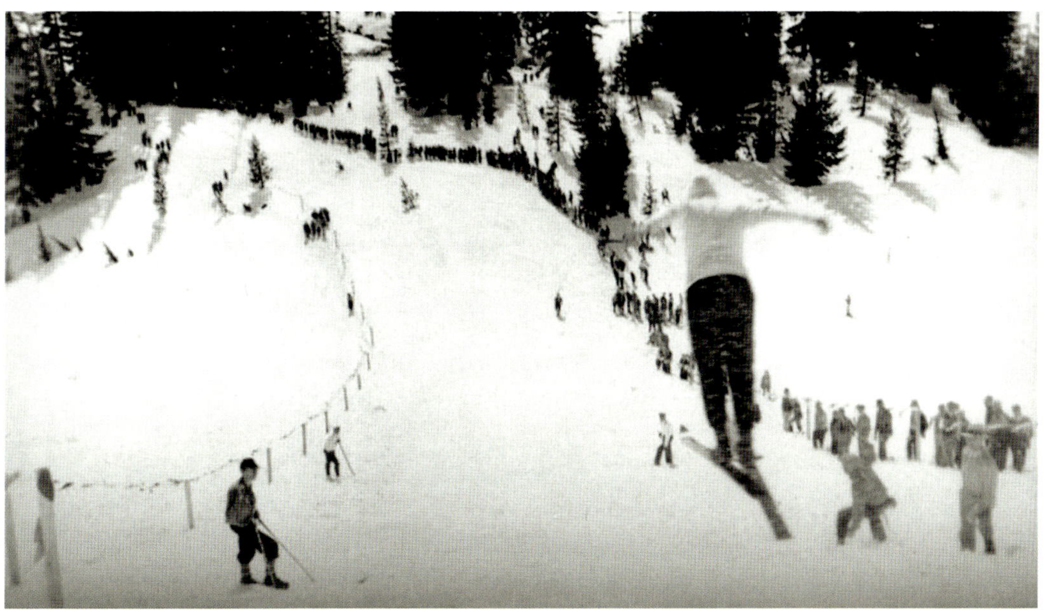

Ski enthusiasts used to enjoy the ski jump at Crater Lake. It was located adjacent to the present-day Annie Creek Sno-Park. The record ski jump of all time was 151 feet. In 1946, a gasoline-driven ski tow was installed. The rope tow was approximately 900 feet long. It replaced previous rope tows that had not been of such a high caliber.

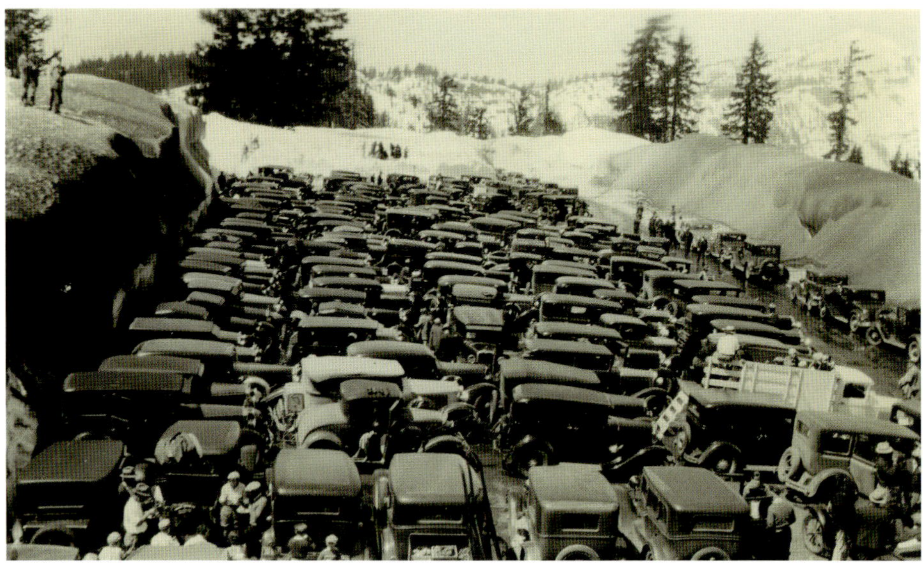

The annual snow carnival used to bring thousands of people to Crater Lake. The activities included snow balling, short races, tobogganing, sleigh rides, barefoot races, sled dog races, and a homing pigeon race. There was also a dance held in the Community House. An estimated 3,500 spectators enjoyed the events in 1931. That number climbed to an estimated 4,000 people in 1933.

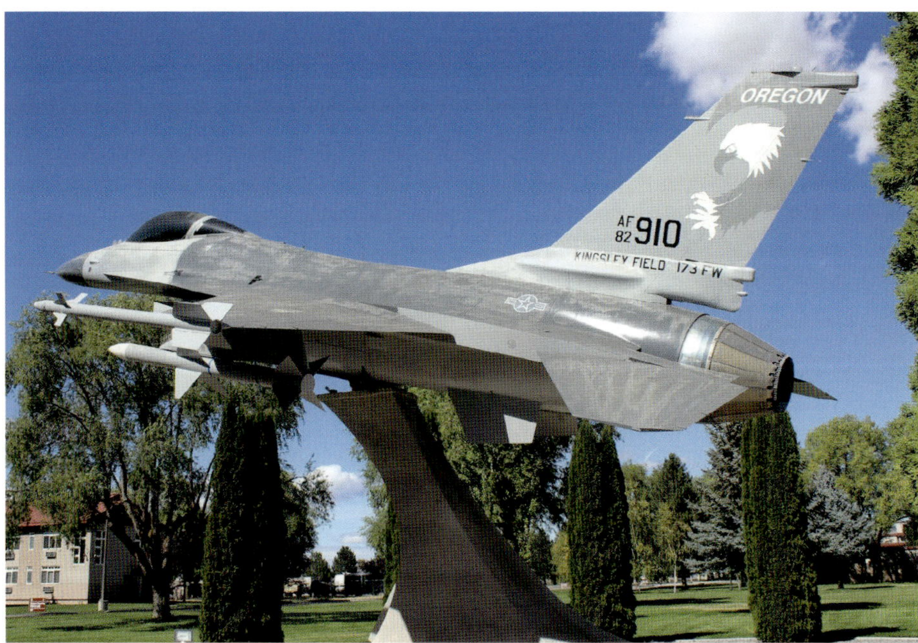

Klamath Falls Airport was constructed in 1928 at a cost of $50,000. During World War II, the airport was used as a Naval Air Station (NAS Klamath Falls.) When the war ended, the airport was transferred back to a civilian airport. In 1954, the airport was selected as a U.S. Air Force Base. It was named for David Kingsley, a war hero from World War II.

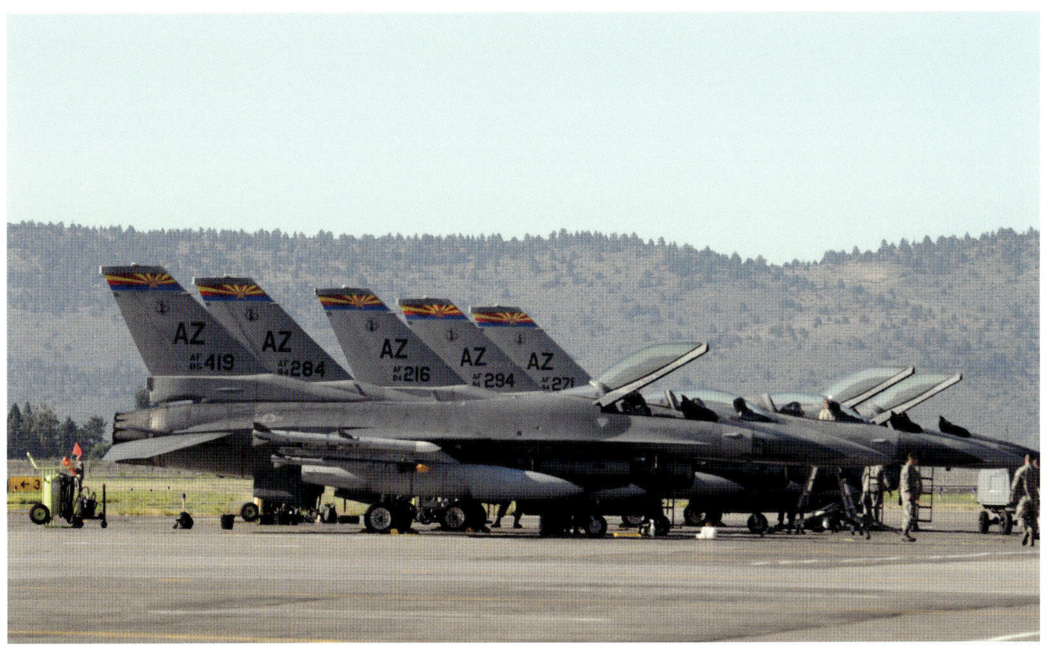

In 1978, the installation was transferred to the Oregon Air National Guard. It has been operated by the Oregon Air National Guard since then.

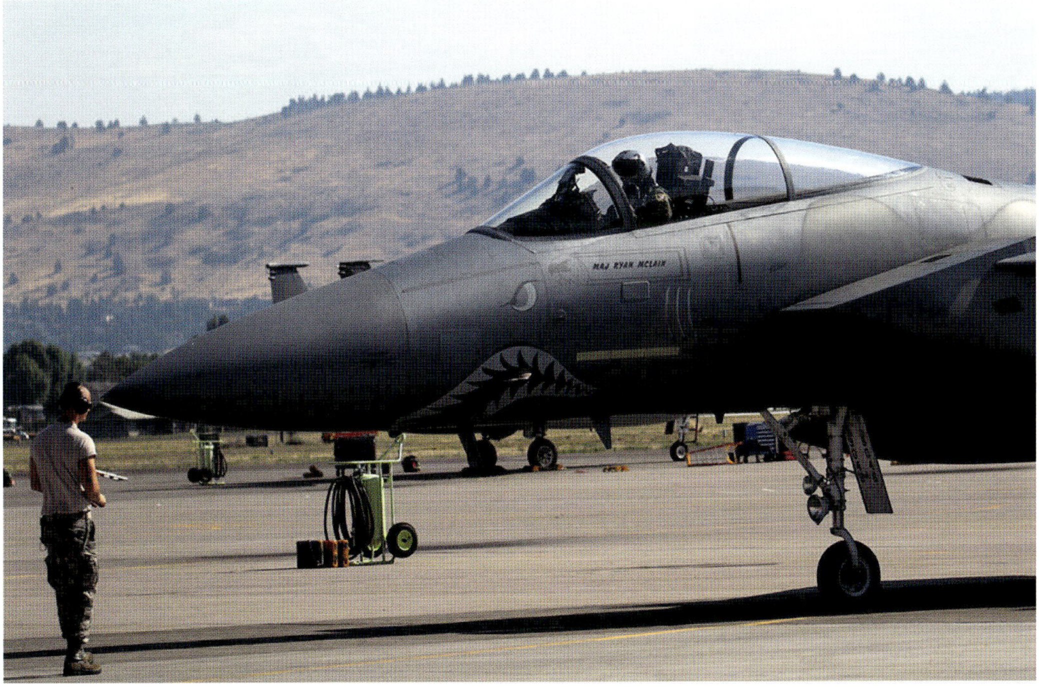

Over the years, many fighter-interceptor squadrons have operated from Kingsley Field.

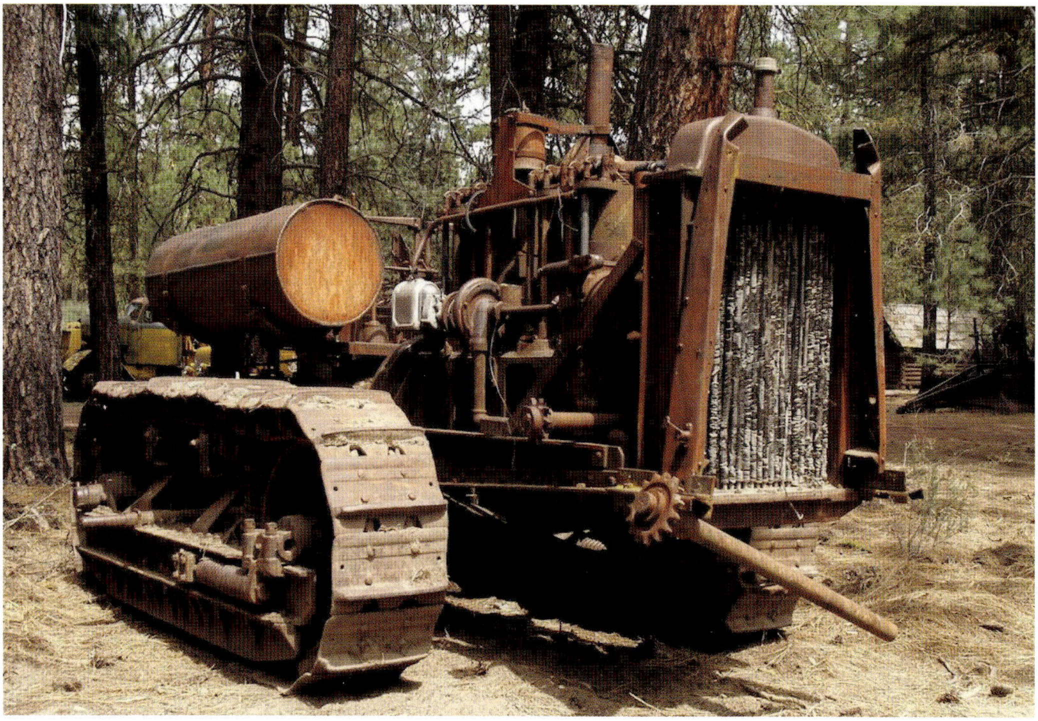

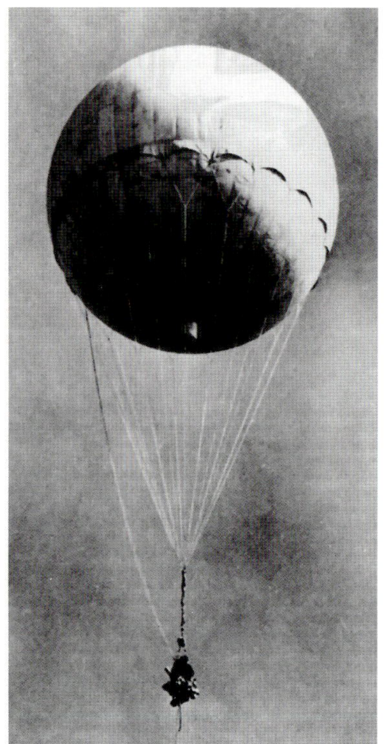

Above: The Collier Memorial State Park has a large display of early-day logging equipment. It was the first logging museum in Oregon. Some of the equipment dates to the late 1800s.

Left: During World War II, the Japanese sent thousands of balloon bombs over the Pacific Ocean with the intent that they would land on American soil and kill civilians. The balloon bombs were approximately seventy feet tall and thirty feet across. The covers were made from layers of paper, to make them as lightweight as possible. Inside was a metal ring holding the hydrogen filled bombs. Most of the balloon bombs sank in the Pacific Ocean.

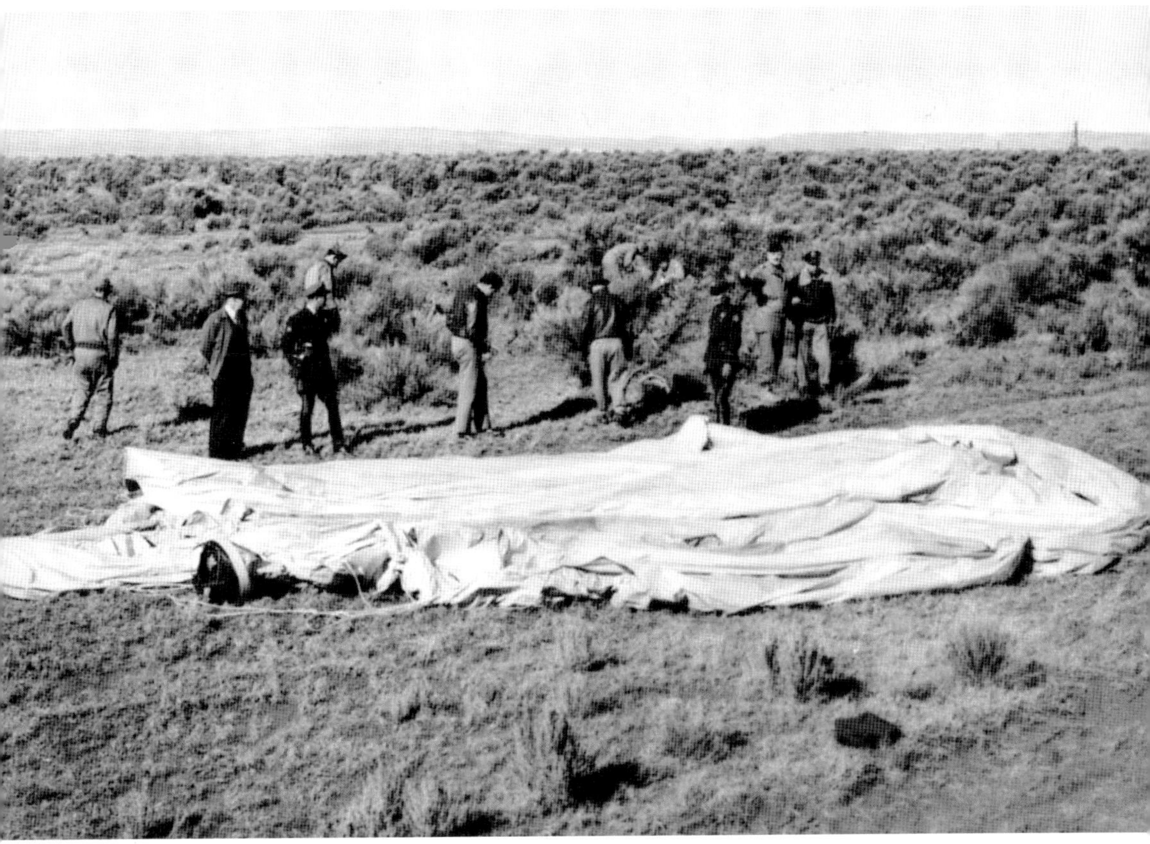

On May 5, 1945, Reverend Archie Mitchell and his wife, Elsie, who was pregnant with their first child, went on a picnic with five children from their church. When they reached Gearhart Mountain, Reverend Mitchell let them out of the car while he went to find a parking spot. Minutes later, they called out to him to let him know they found a strange object on the ground. It turned out to be a balloon bomb.

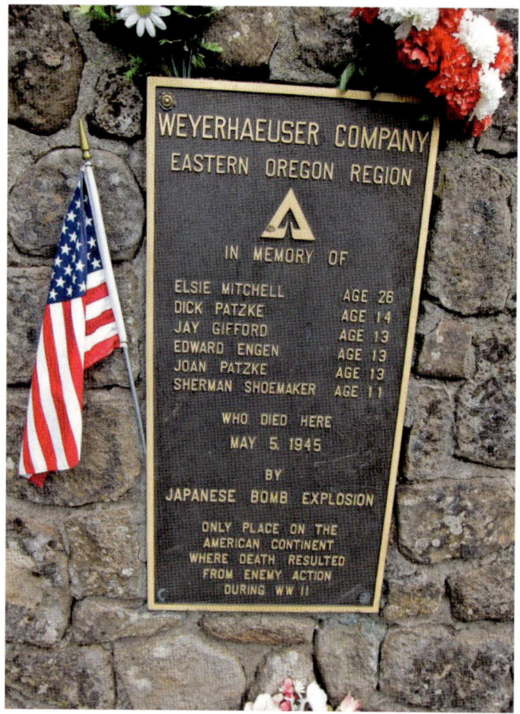

Left: Elsie, her unborn baby, and the five children were killed instantly. It is thought that someone touched the balloon bomb, causing it to explode. The children who died ranged in age from eleven to fourteen. They were the only casualties on the mainland United States during World War II as a result of enemy action.

Below: The area where the balloon bomb exploded was dedicated as the Mitchell Monument. A Ponderosa pine tree still bears shrapnel from the explosion. At the time of the explosion, the U.S. government chose to censor the story. They were concerned that if the Japanese learned that one of their balloon bombs had been successful, they would send even more.

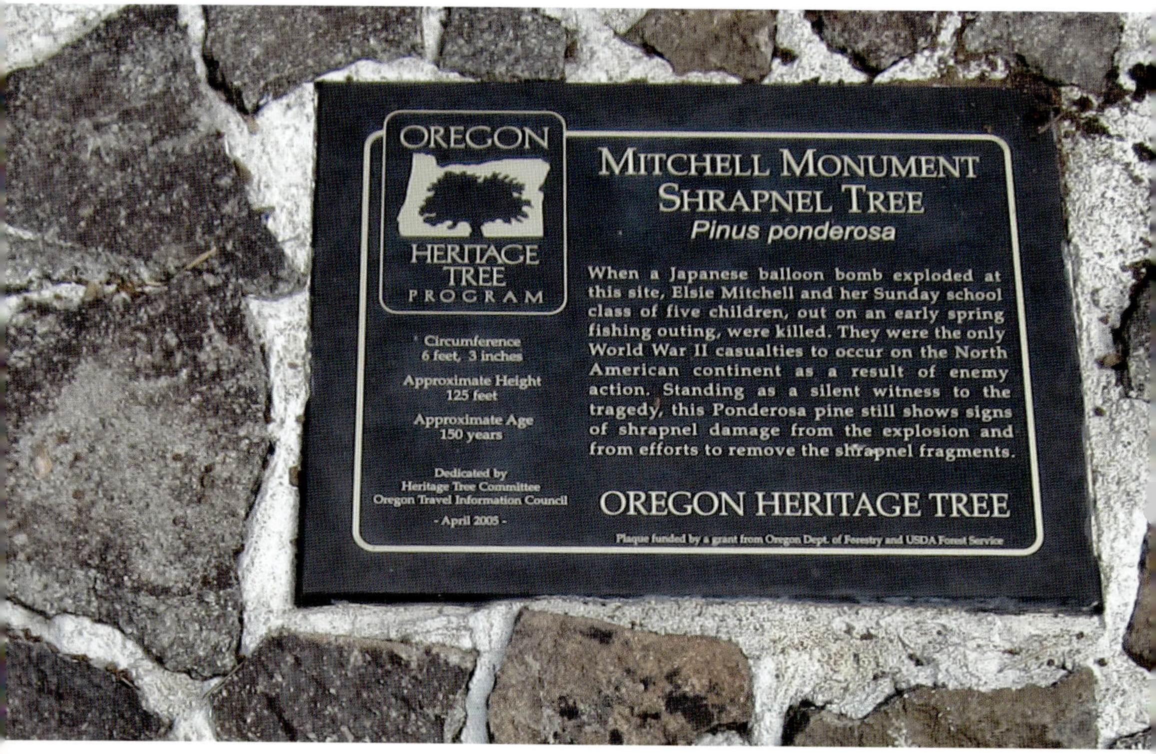

3

Jackson, Josephine, and Douglas Counties

Jackson County was named for President Andrew Jackson. Jackson had been a general in the U.S. Army, a senator, and a representative prior to becoming the seventh president of the United States. The original layout of Jackson County was considerably larger than it is today. Portions of Jackson County were distributed amongst neighboring counties.

Josephine County was named for Josephine Rollins. She was born in Morgan County, Illinois, in 1833 to Lloyd and Katherine Rollins. She came overland with her father in 1850. They were headed for the California Gold Rush but made the decision to winter in Oregon. The following spring, they left Oregon City to head to California. A group of Indians informed them of some gold diggings on a nearby river. They did find gold in the river, which is named for Josephine. In 1913, Josephine wrote a letter to George H. Parker of Josephine County to answer his questions about her time in the area. In part she replied, "I was honored by having the county named for me, but by whom I know not. I was married to Julius Ort in Colusa County, California, in 1854. In 1863, we moved to Sonoma County, where we have lived and made our home ever since."

In 1851, the territorial legislature created Umpqua County. The local river had already been named Umpqua and there was a local Indian tribe by that name. However, Umpqua County was short lived. The following year, the territorial legislature took part of the county and created Douglas County. Other portions of Umpqua County were distributed to Coos County. The newly formed Douglas County was named for Stephen Arnold Douglas, a senator from Illinois who ran for president of the United States in 1860.

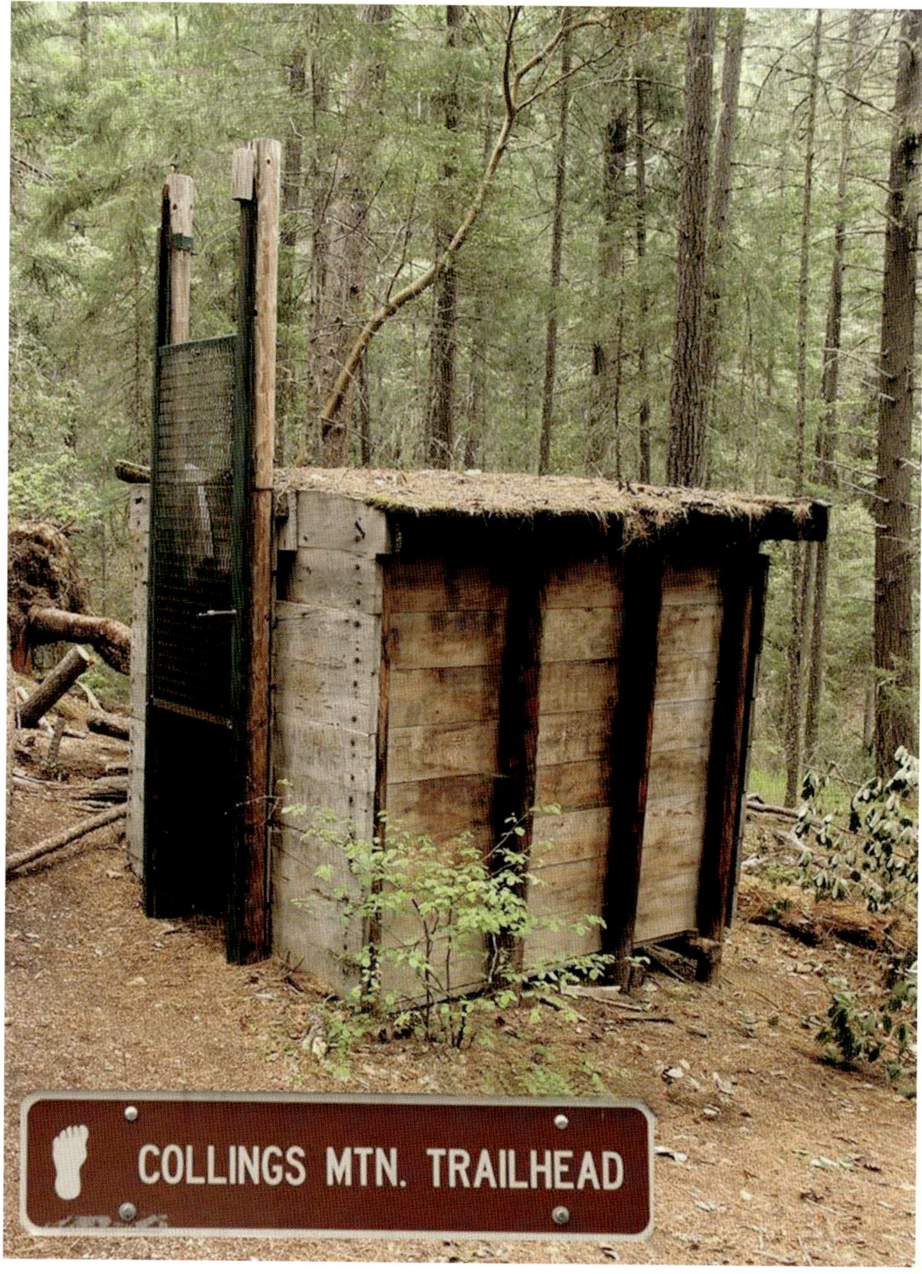

The Bigfoot trap located near the Applegate Lake is said to be the only one in the world. It was built in 1974 by the North American Wildlife Research Team. The trap was constructed of wooden slats that were reinforced with steel bolts and plates. The trap measures ten feet long by ten feet wide. To date there have been no sightings of the elusive Bigfoot, or Sasquatch, as he is sometimes referred to.

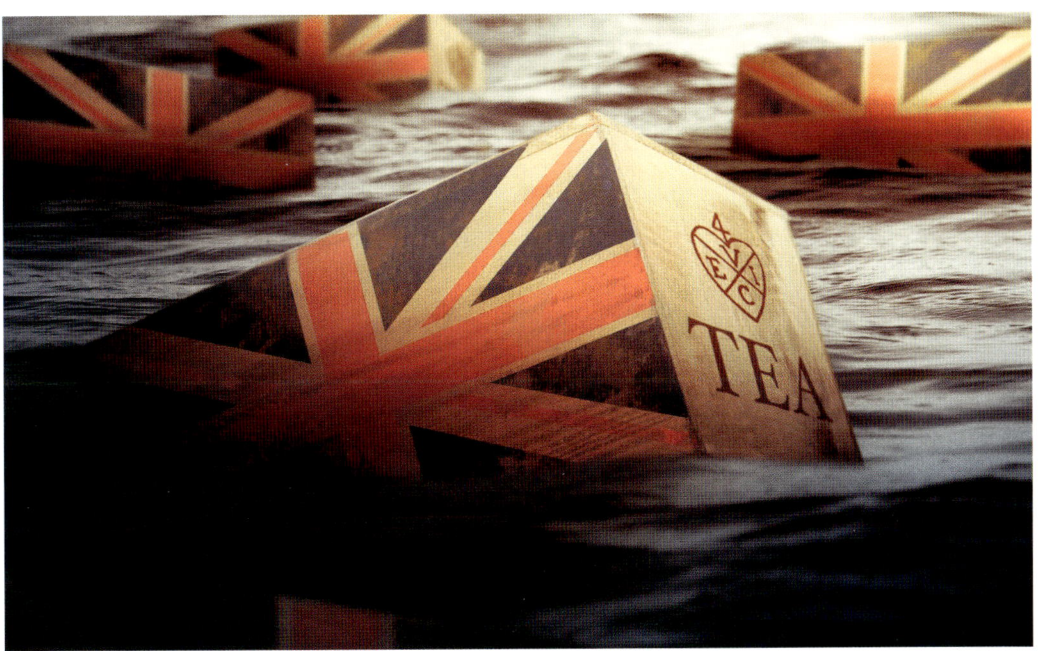

In October 1961, delegates from Jackson County visited Great Britain. Prior to the trip, they decided that if they were going to go to Great Britain, they should pay their share of the Boston Tea Party debt. Based on the population of Jackson County at the time, they concluded that their share of the debt would be $1.96. Once in Great Britain, they presented the money to the tea firm of Davidson and Newman.

The co-founder of Nike, Bill Bowerman, attended high school in Medford. He played football and basketball. He attended college at the University of Oregon. After graduating, he worked as a coach at Medford High School from 1935-1941. He served in the U.S. Army during World War II. When the war ended, he returned to his coaching job at Medford High School. In 1947, Bill accepted a coaching job at the University of Oregon.

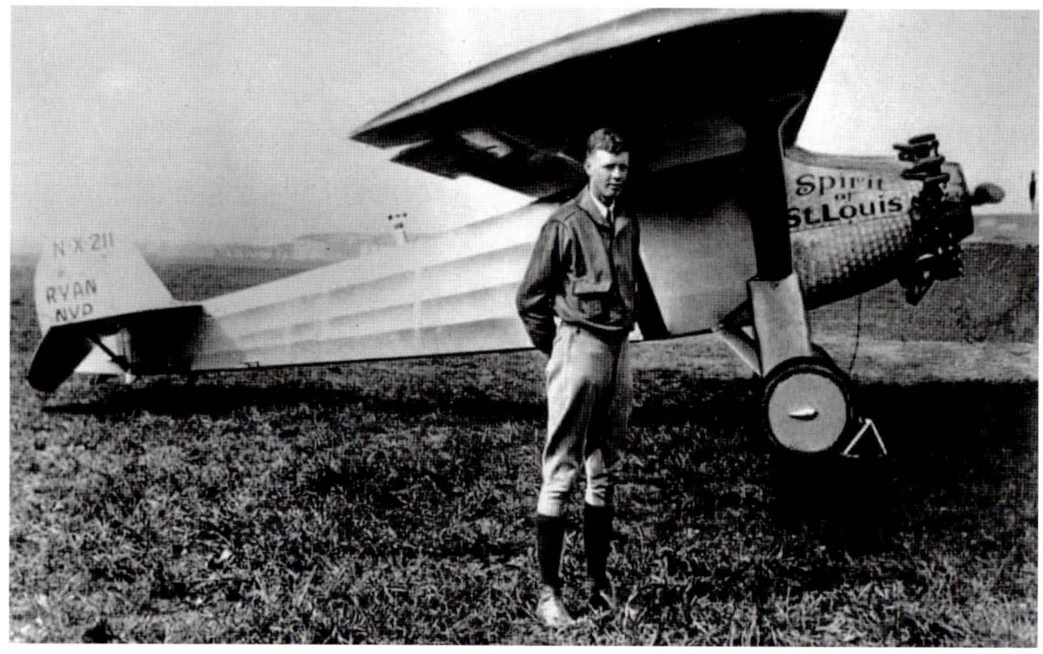

This photograph of Charles Lindbergh was taken shortly after he touched down in Paris after making his famous non-stop flight from New York in 1927. The following year, Charles touched down in Medford. In 1939, he once again touched down in Medford, this time to refuel his Curtis P-36 Army Air Corps pursuit-interceptor airplane.

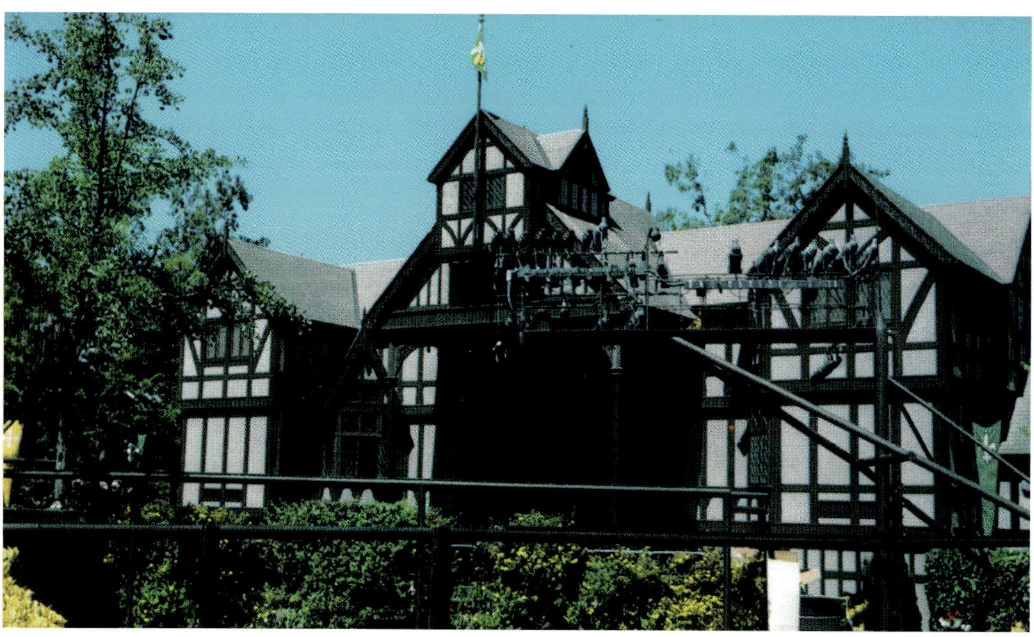

In 1935, Angus Bowmer asked the Ashland City Council for permission to put on three Shakespeare plays.

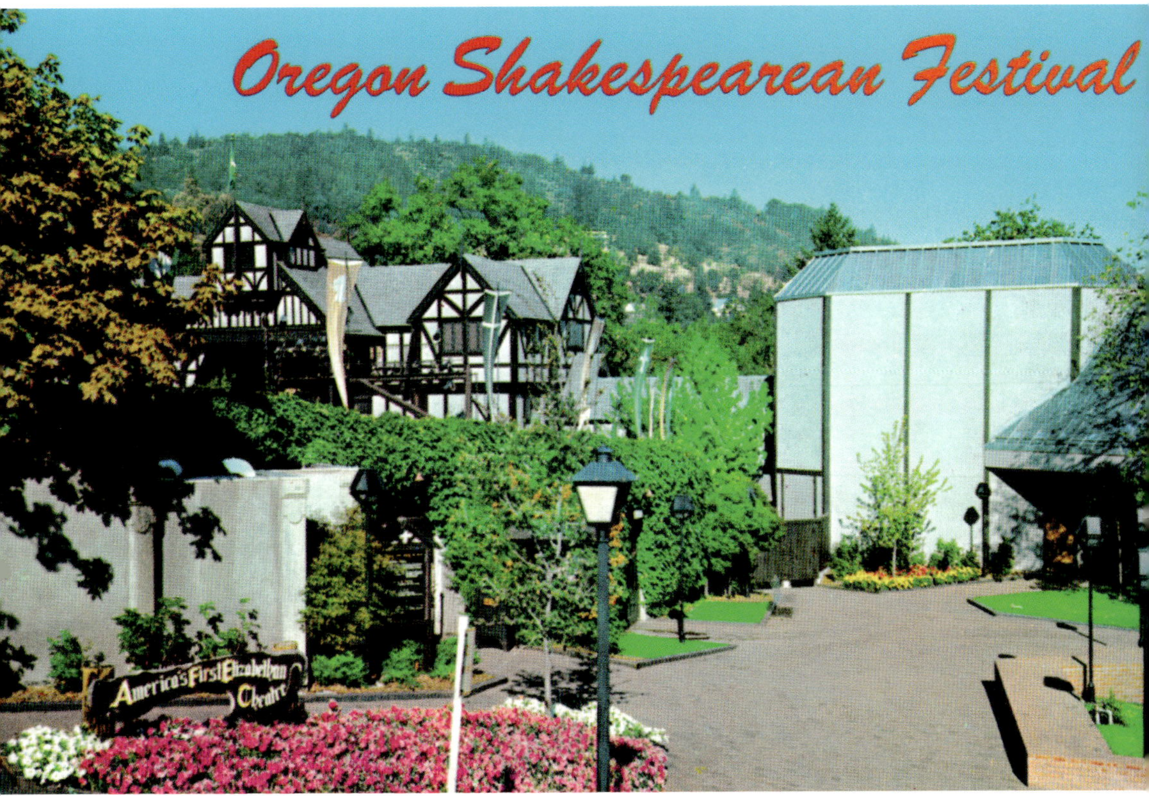

The City Council reluctantly agreed to two plays, but there was a catch. They insisted that he use the stage for boxing matches during the day. They reasoned that the money lost on the Shakespeare plays could be offset by the revenue generated by the boxing matches. As it turned out, the plays offset the revenue loss from the boxing matches.

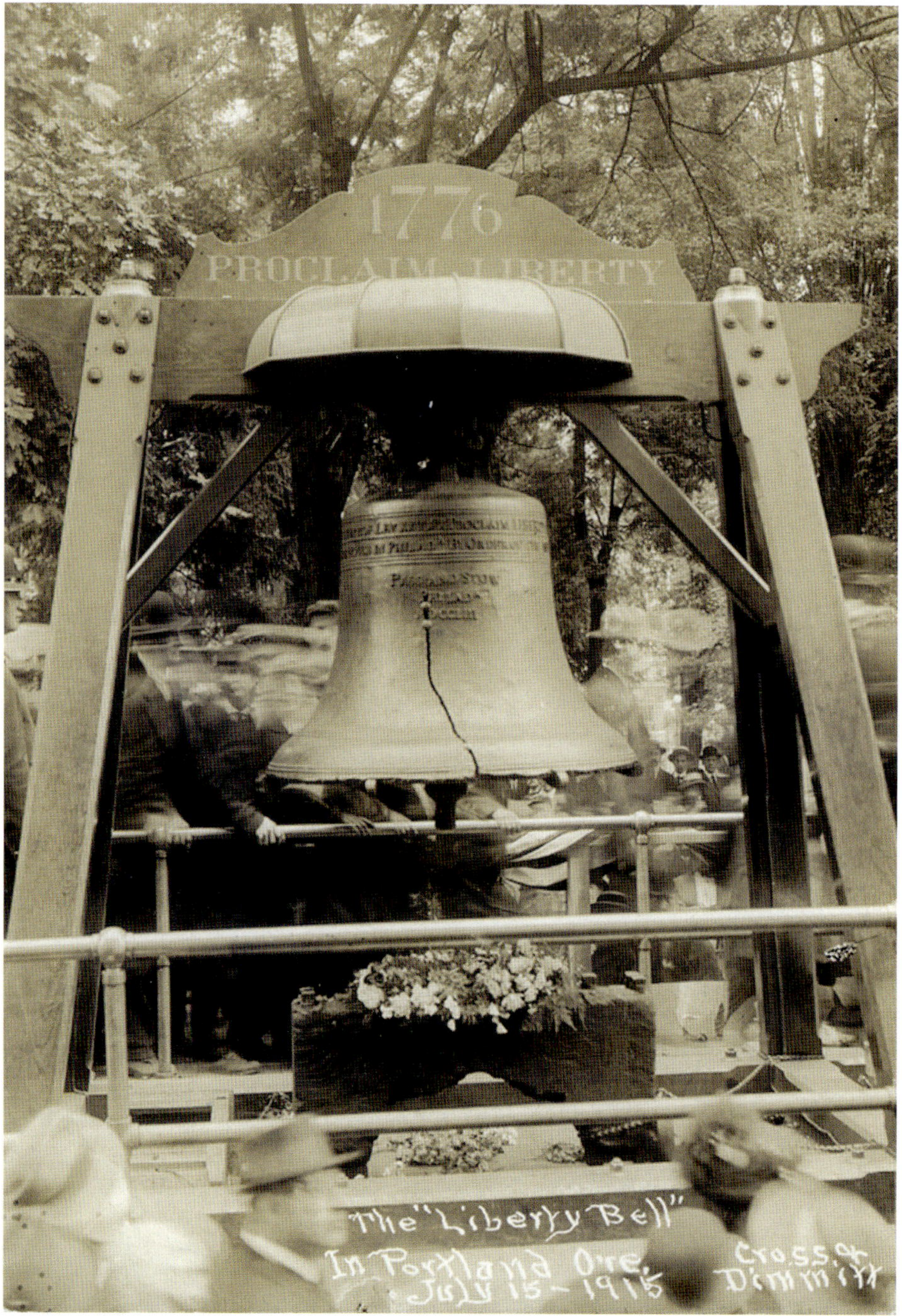

Early on the morning on July 15, 1915, the Liberty Bell passed through the towns of Grants Pass, Medford, and Ashland. Large crowds gathered in each town to celebrate. The Liberty Bell was on a train that had a special gondola decorated in red, white, and blue. The Liberty Bell was on its way to the Panama Pacific Exposition in San Francisco. The Exposition was held to celebrate the opening of the Panama Canal.

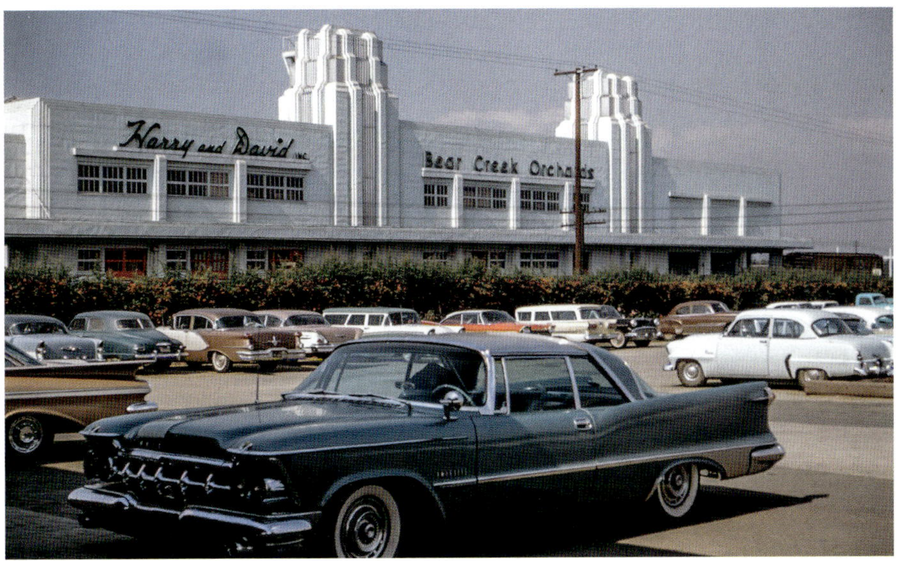

Harry and David was founded in 1910 in Medford when Samuel Rosenberg bought the Bear Creek Orchards. He began selling the pears produced at the orchard. When Samuel died in 1914, his sons, Harry and David, took over the business. They began marketing the pears as Royal Riviera and selling them throughout Europe and America. During World War II, they took on the surname of their stepfather, Holmes, in order to be accepted in the business world.

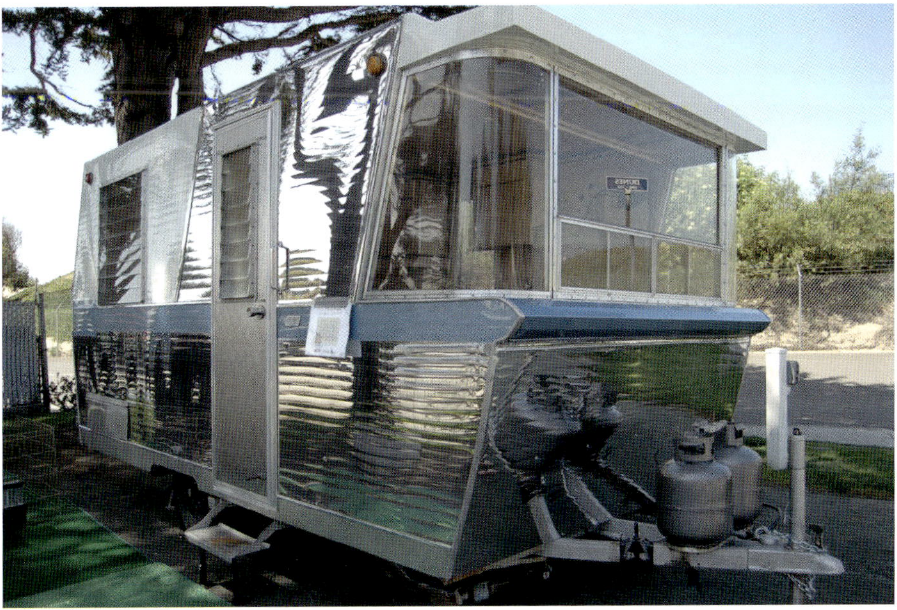

Fruit baskets are synonymous with Harry and David, but in 1959, they decided they should have an off-season business in order to keep their employees on the payroll year-round. They went into the travel trailer manufacturing business. They hired Chuck Pelly, who was well renowned for designing racecars. They created the Holiday House trailer. These were the first trailers made of aluminum.

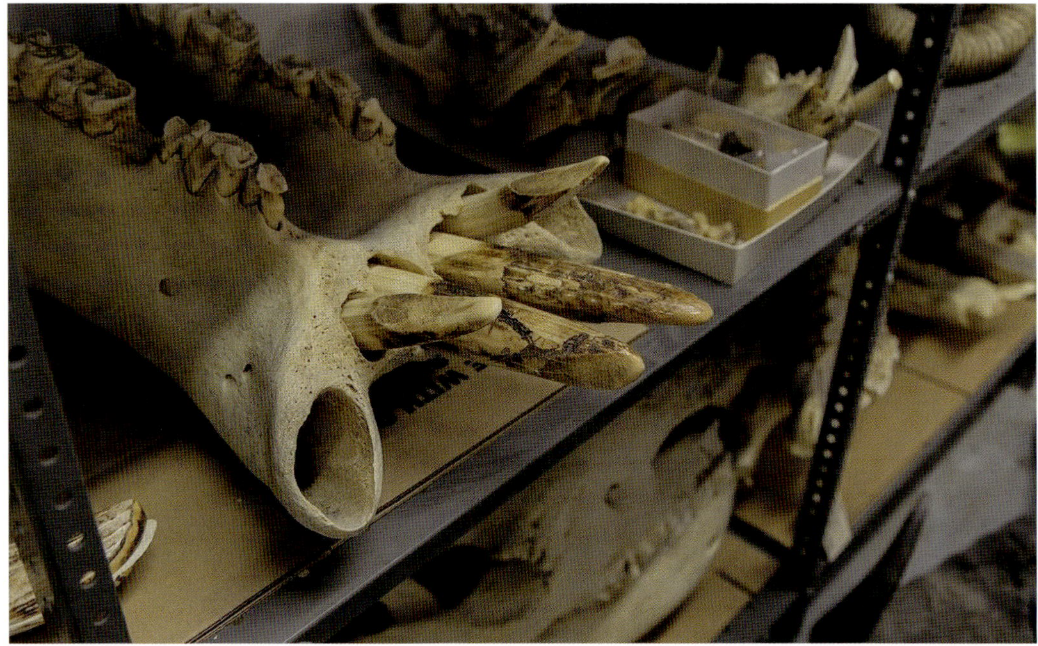

The U.S. Fish and Wildlife Service Forensic Laboratory is located in Ashland. It is the only one in the world. The forensic laboratory opened in 1989. Since that time, they have made a huge difference in fighting crime against poachers and animal traffickers. They use scientific methods and equipment to link a suspect and a victim to a crime.

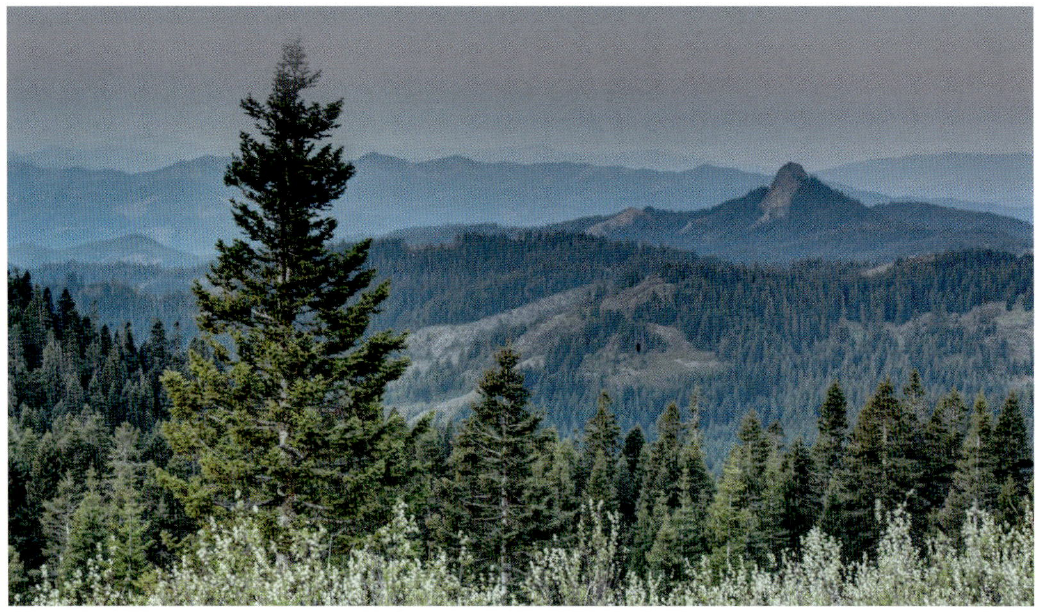

The Cascade-Siskiyou National Monument provides a scenic backdrop to the Cascade, Klamath, and Siskiyou Mountain ranges. It is home to bears, deer, mountain lions, birds, and small mammals.

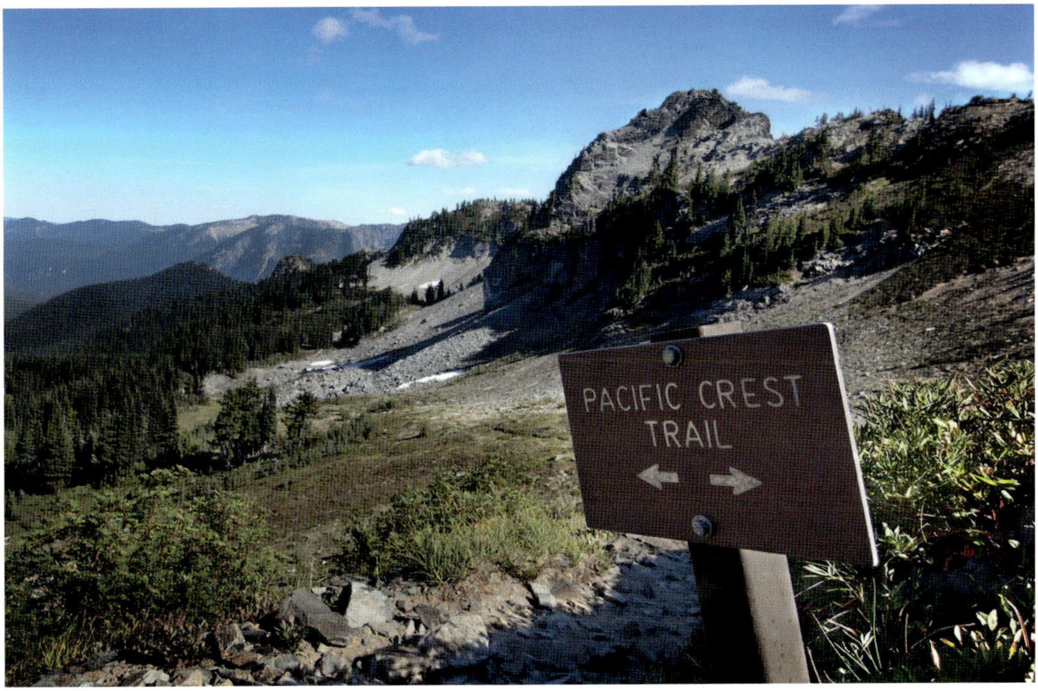

The Pacific Crest Trail begins at the California-Mexico border and ends at the Washington-Canada border. Part of the trail passes through Oregon, beginning near Mount Ashland. The entire trail covers 2,650 miles.

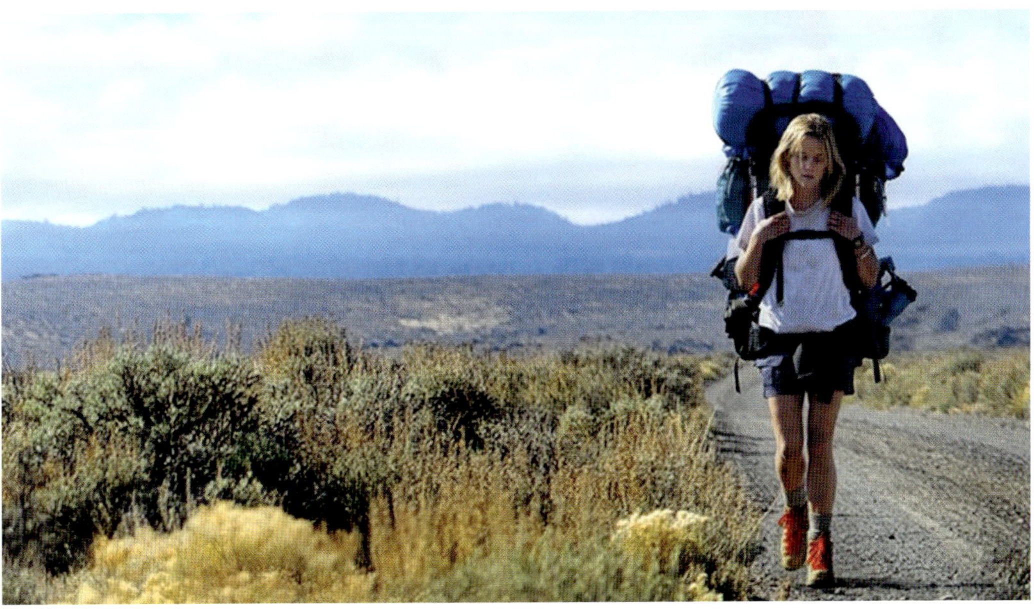

A portion of the movie *Wild*, starring Reese Witherspoon, was filmed in Ashland as she made her way along the Pacific Crest Trail.

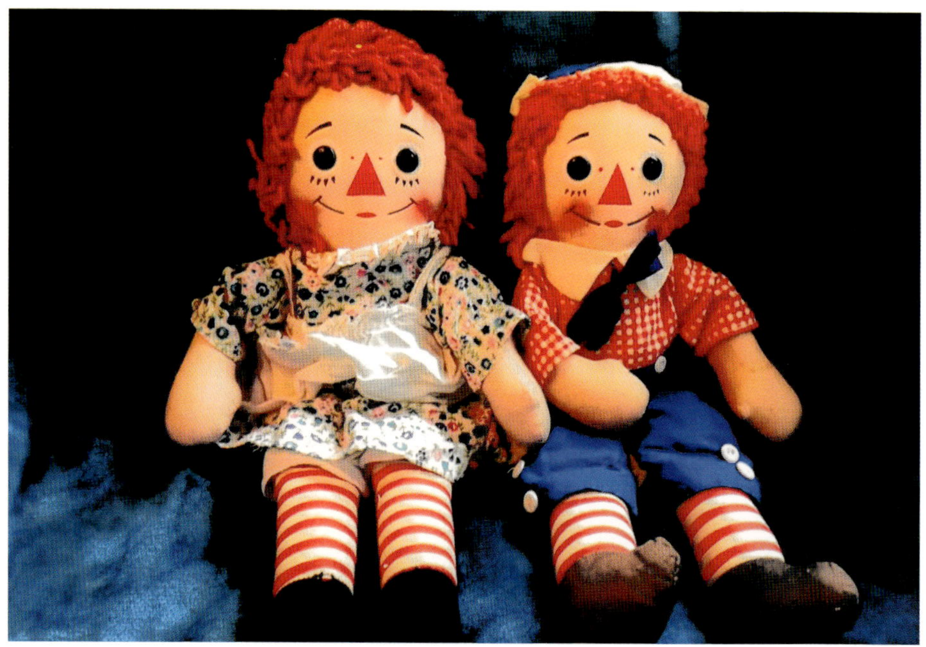

The creator of Raggedy Ann and Raggedy Andy, John Barton Gruelle, lived in Ashland for a year during the 1920s. The house that he and his family rented still stands today.

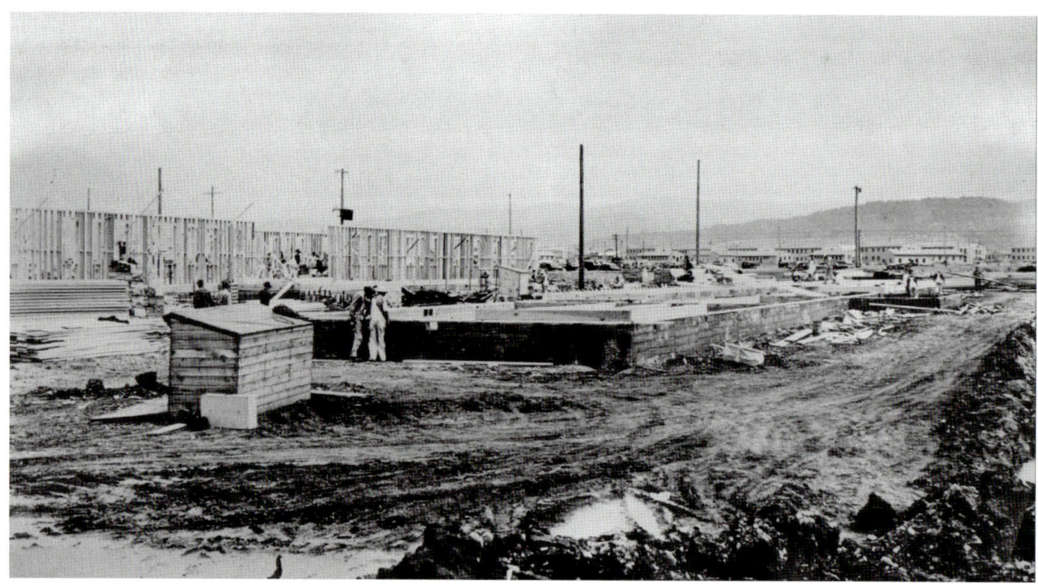

The population of Jackson County increased seemingly overnight when it was announced that Jackson County had been selected as a military cantonment. Pearl Harbor had been attacked weeks earlier and the U.S. government needed to train troops prior to being sent overseas. Jackson County had sent promotional materials to the U.S. government the previous year in the hopes of being selected for a cantonment.

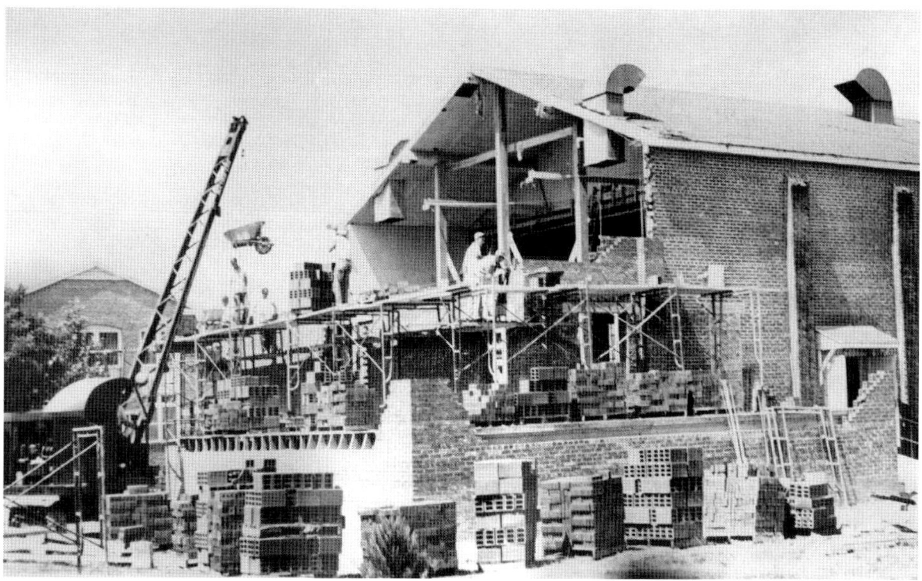

Gigantic light towers run by gasoline generators were used during the night so that construction crews could work twenty-four hours a day. Equipment was brought in from out of state. Workers lived on site in "tent cities" consisting of a wood floor with wood sides and a tarp overhead. Local residents were asked to rent out any extra space they had to accommodate workers.

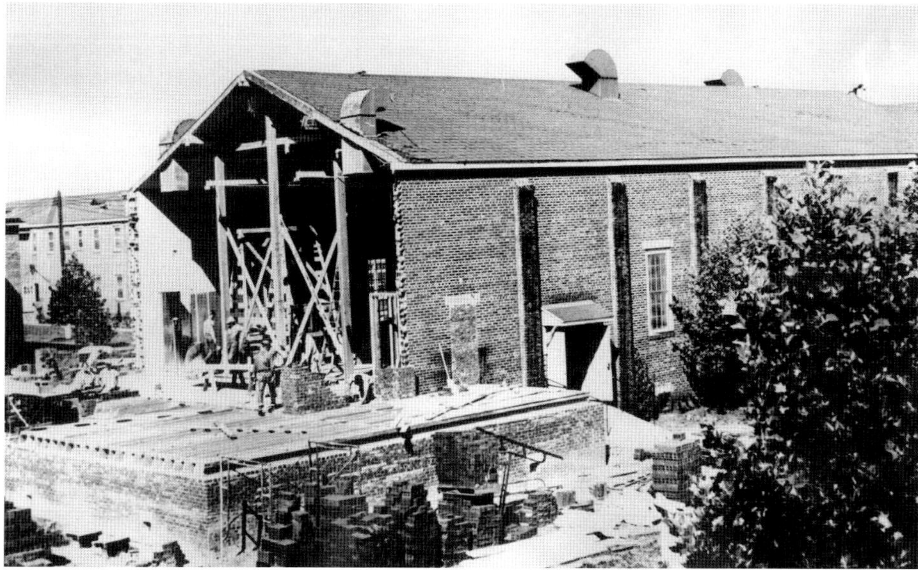

Construction was completed in six months. The first troops of the 91st Fir Tree Division arrived in the summer of 1942. Camp White was officially dedicated on September 15, 1942. It was named for Major General George A. White, who commanded the 41st Infantry Division of the Oregon National Guard from 1930-1941.

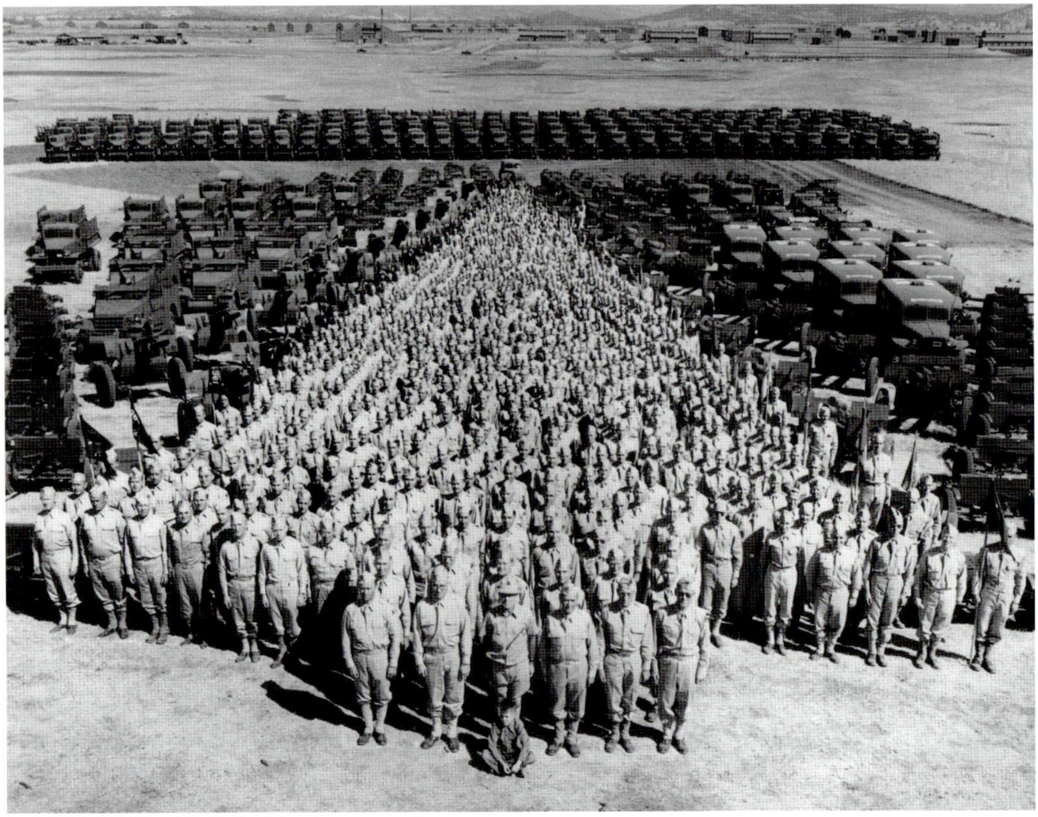

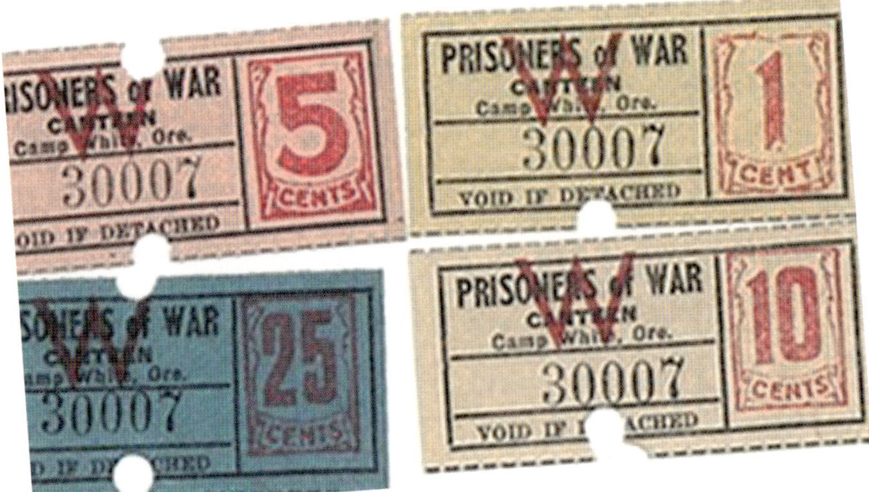

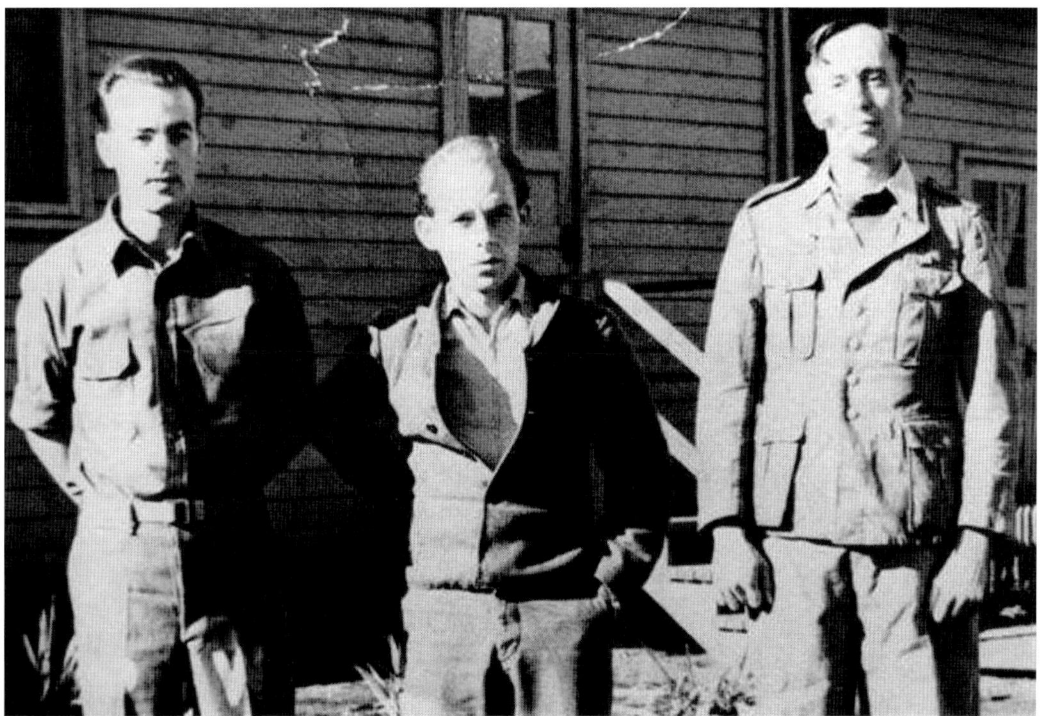

In 1943, the government decided that the POWs could work in industries that did not compete with American workers. Many of the POWs worked in the local orchards and were paid 80 cents per day.

Opposite above: More than 40,000 soldiers trained at Camp White. The 91st Division was designated as a triangular division, meaning that the infantry, artillery, medical staff, and engineers were all under one commander. The division was originally activated in 1917 at Fort Lewis, Washington, prior to World War I. Their slogan was "Powder River, Let'er Buck." Their emblem was a western fir tree.

Opposite below: In 1942, the U.S. Government began detaining Germans as Prisoners of War (POWs). A total of 1,600 Germans were held at Camp White. The facility had several compounds including barracks, a mess hall, storage buildings, and offices.

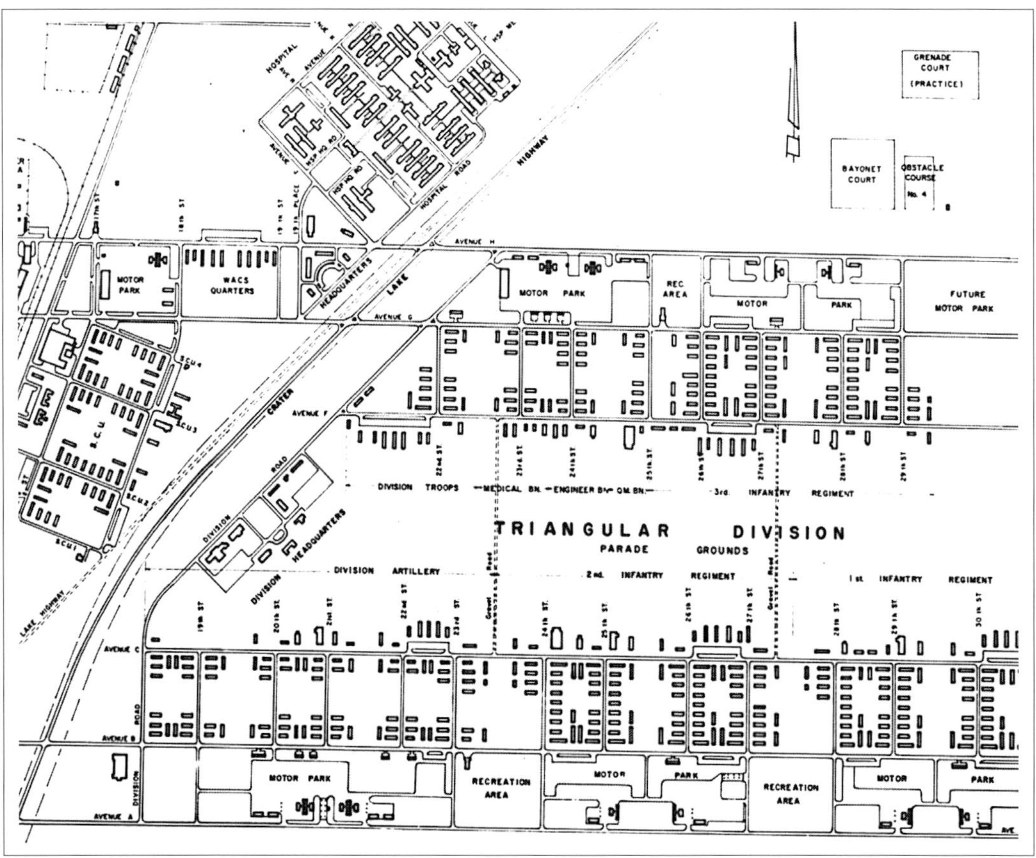

In 1946, the U.S. Government's War Assets Administration placed Camp White on the surplus list and ordered that 1,185 of the buildings be auctioned. They also put the electrical, plumbing, heating, refrigeration systems, and office furniture on the auction block. Many of the buildings were sold locally and used for homes and businesses. A small percentage of the original buildings remain at the Camp White site and have served various purposes over the years.

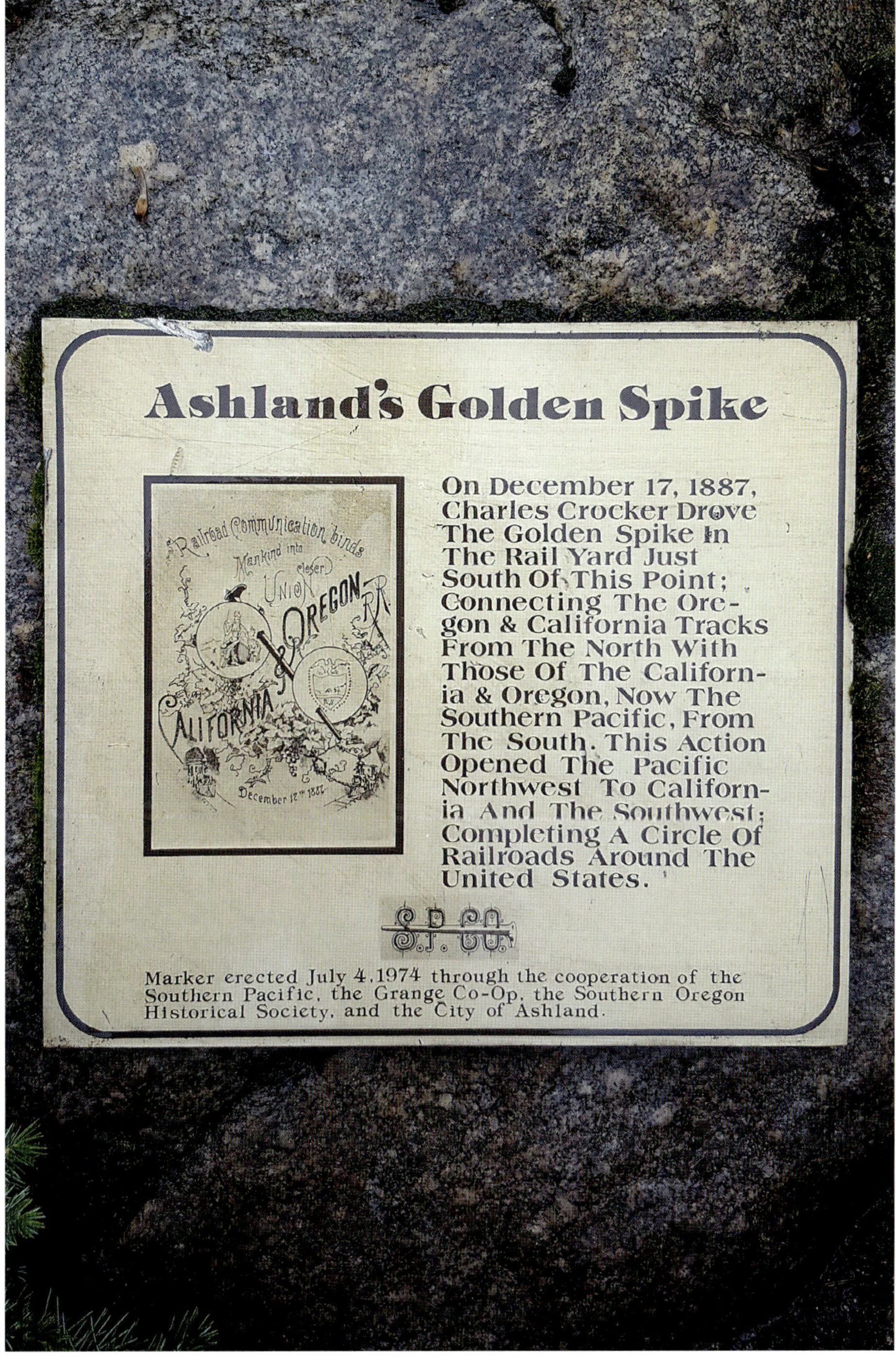

On a cold, rainy day on December 17, 1887, officials gathered in Ashland for the golden spike ceremony. With the driving of the golden spike, the railroads circled the entire United States for the first time.

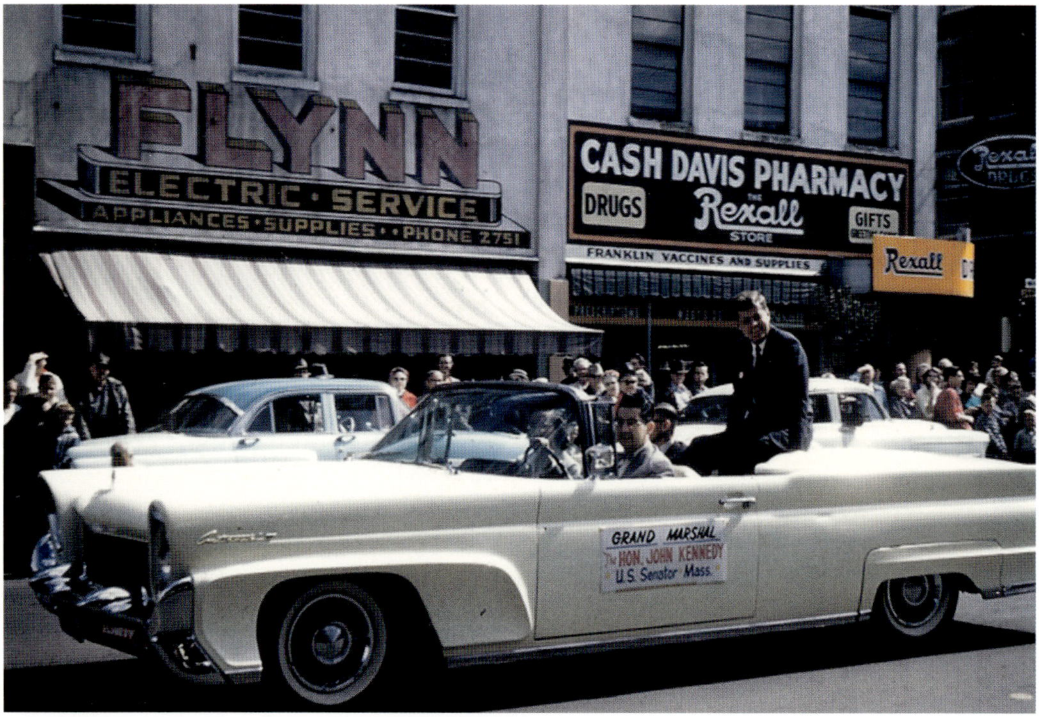

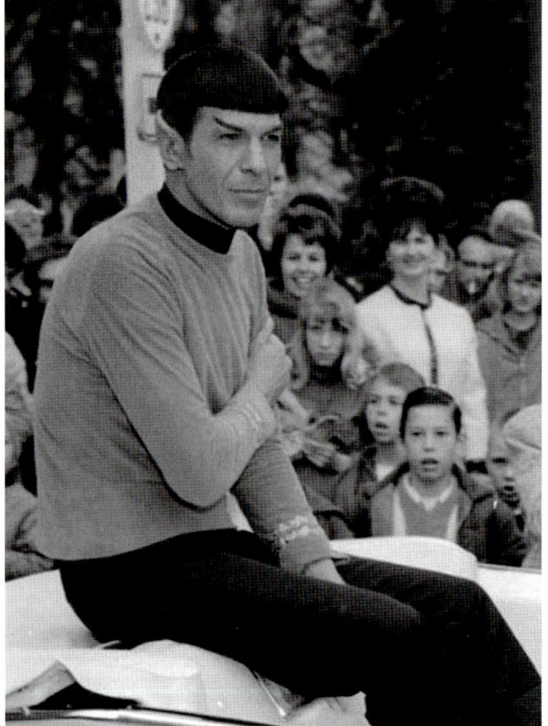

Above: In 1960, while campaigning for the Democratic presidential nomination, Massachusetts senator, John F. Kennedy, served as the grand marshal of the Pear Blossom Parade. Local resident Wally Watkins is pictured driving his own cream colored 1959 Lincoln Continental Mark III. Kennedy later sent Watkins an invitation to his inauguration. During Kennedy's time in Oregon, he also made stops in Portland and Eugene.

Left: The one and only time that Spock appeared in costume in public was in Medford. In 1967, the television network sent him to Medford for publicity. He reigned as the Grand Marshall of the Pear Blossom Parade. In his memoir, *I Am Spock*, he described that the mob scene at Alba Park was so huge that he feared someone might be crushed to death. He said the local police had to protect him from the crowd.

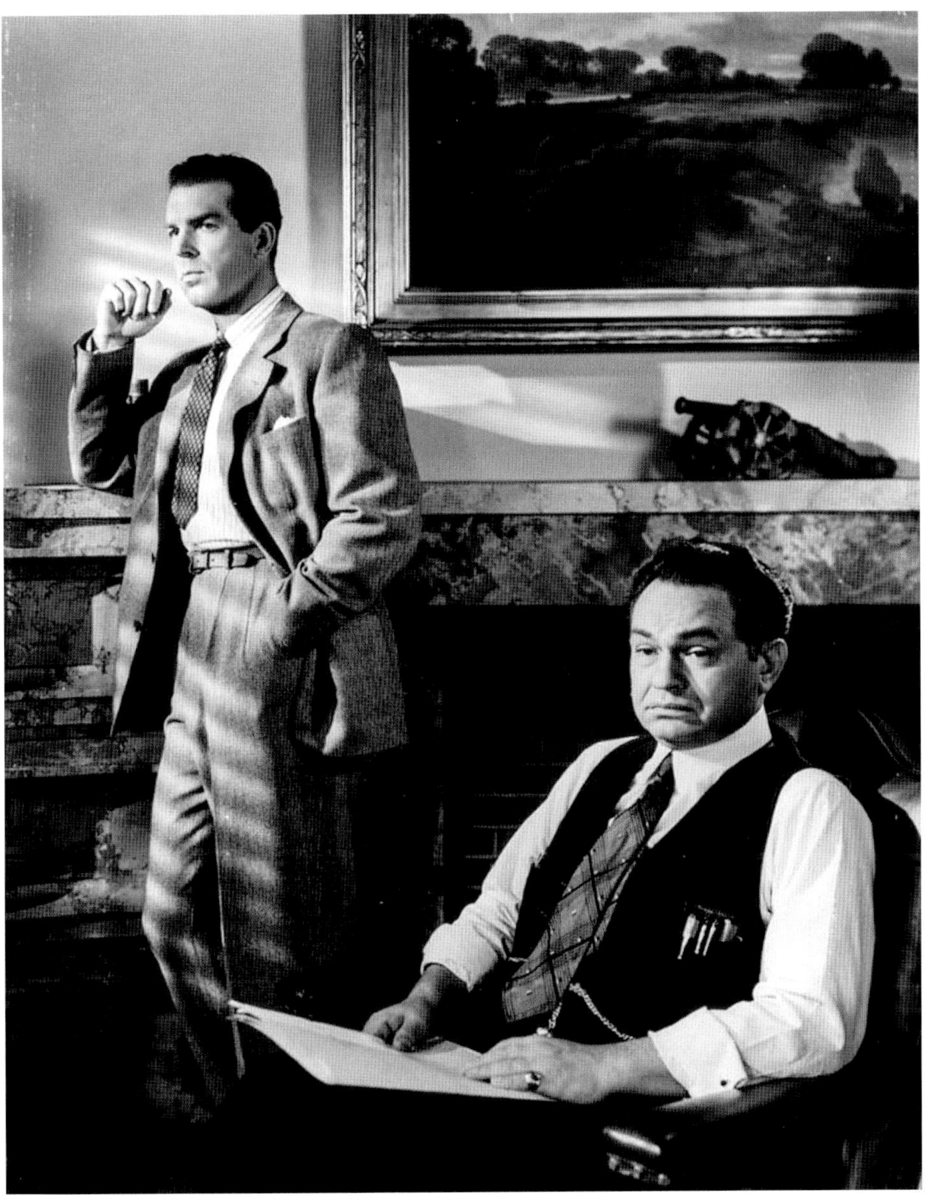

In the 1944 film noir, *Double Indemnity*, Barton Keyes asks Mr. Jackson, "Have you made up your mind?" Mr. Jackson replies, "Mr. Keyes, I'm a Medford man—Medford, Oregon. Up in Medford, we take our time making up our minds." Keyes is quick to reply, "Well, we're not in Medford, we're in a hurry." When asked if he would swear that the man in question was on the train, Mr. Jackson says, "I'm a Medford man. Medford, Oregon."

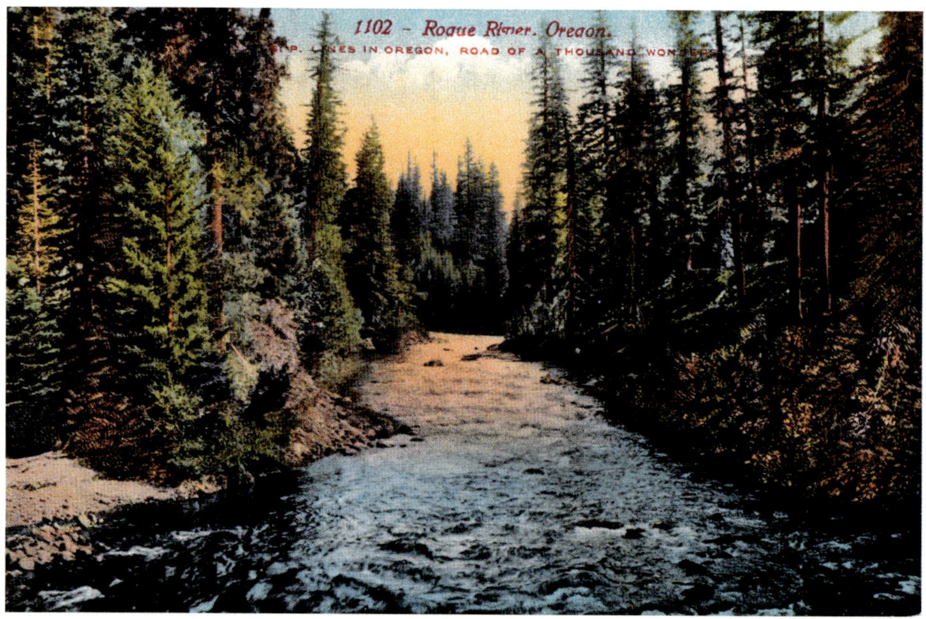

The Rogue River has been the backdrop for many movies. Just a few of the movies filmed on the Rogue River include *The Rogue River*, *Rooster Cogburn*, and *The River Wild*. An episode of the television show, *Gunsmoke*, was also filmed on the Rogue River.

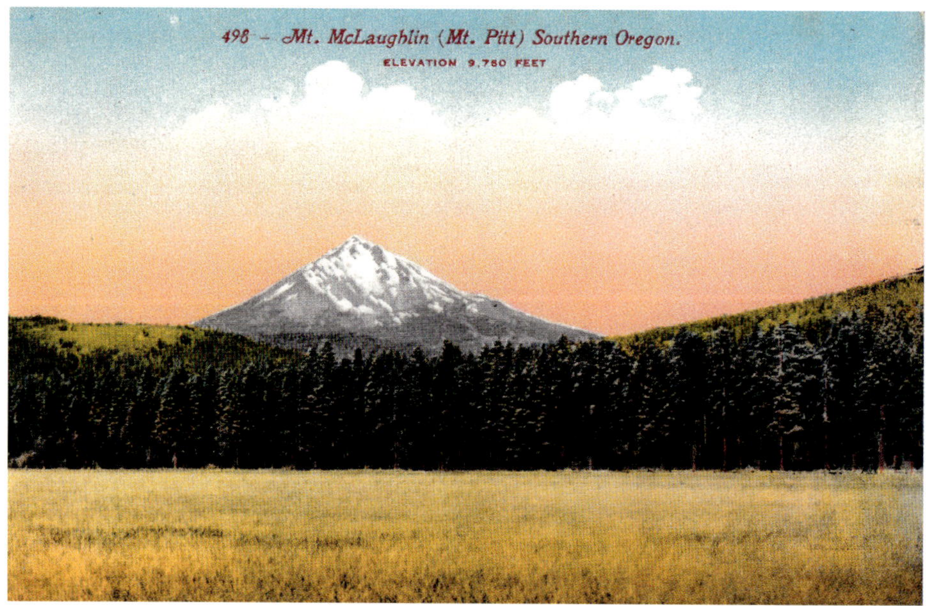

The local Indians looked to Mount McLaughlin each spring. When the snow melted to the point that angel wings appeared, they knew the river would be teaming with salmon. Mount McLaughlin was originally named Mount Pitt.

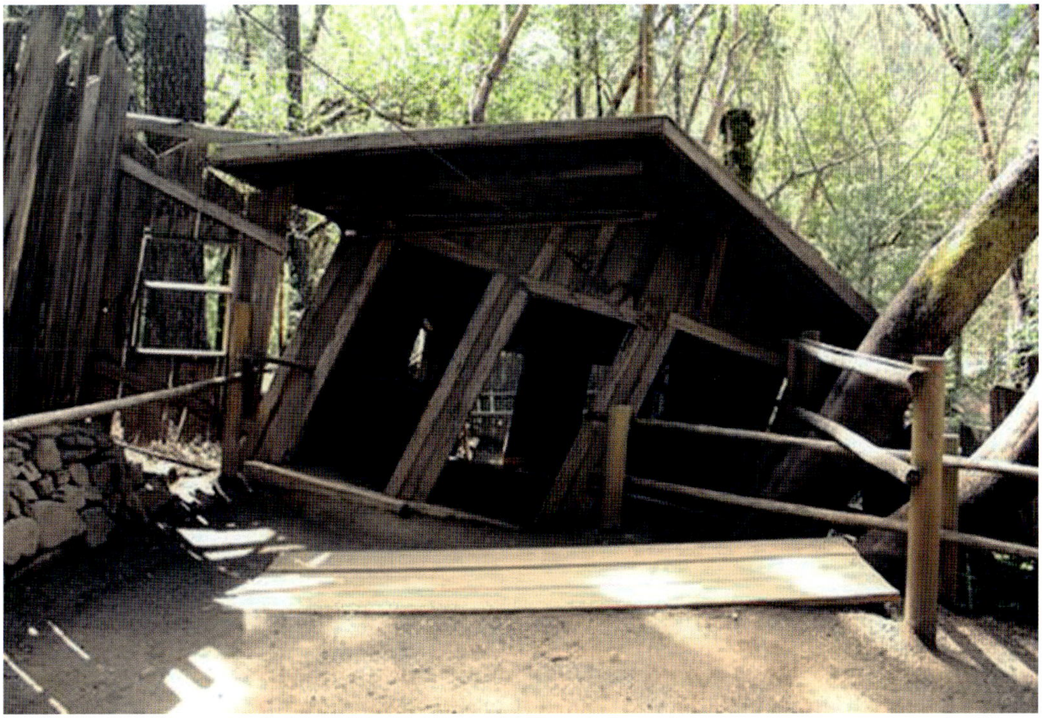

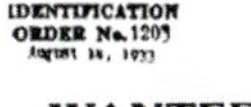

The Oregon Vortex and the House of Mystery opened to the public in 1930. Strange phenomena and paranormal optical illusions greet those who visit.

In 1933, Machine Gun Kelly and his partner, Albert Bates, kidnapped oil tycoon Charles Urschel in Oklahoma and held him for ransom. The $200,000 ransom was paid. Months later, more than $5,000 of that ransom money turned up in Medford. Police made contact with Alvin Scott, who was in possession of the money. The Department of Justice searched his house and located a sound-proof room that they believed could have been used for a future kidnapping.

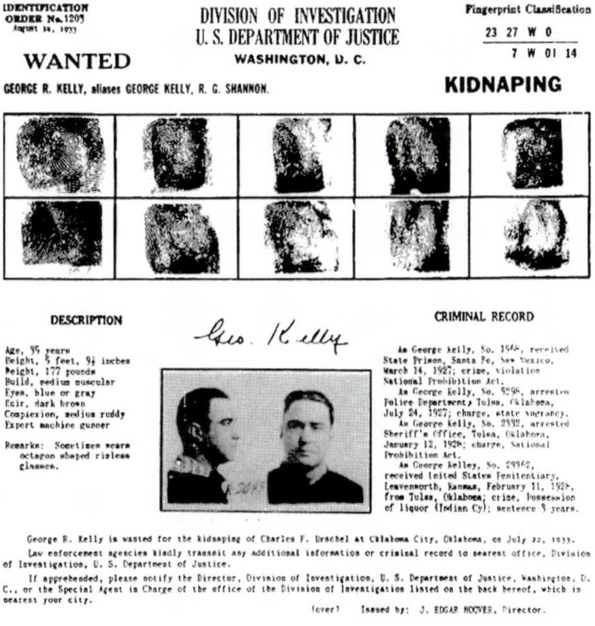

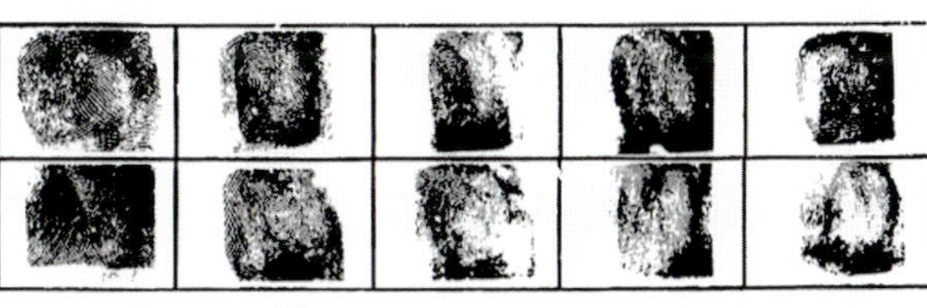

IDENTIFICATION ORDER No. 1205
August 14, 1933

DIVISION OF INVESTIGATION
U. S. DEPARTMENT OF JUSTICE
WASHINGTON, D. C.

WANTED

Fingerprint Classification
23 27 W O
7 W 01 14

KIDNAPING

GEORGE R. KELLY, aliases GEORGE KELLY, R. G. SHANNON.

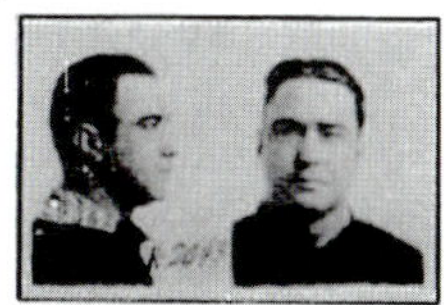

DESCRIPTION

Age, 35 years
Height, 5 feet, 9½ inches
Weight, 177 pounds
Build, medium muscular
Eyes, blue or gray
Hair, dark brown
Complexion, medium ruddy
Expert machine gunner

Remarks: Sometimes wears octagon shaped rimless glasses.

CRIMINAL RECORD

As George Kelly, No. 1945, received State Prison, Santa Fe, New Mexico, March 14, 1927; crime, violation National Prohibition Act.
As George Kelly, No. 5298, arrested Police Department, Tulsa, Oklahoma, July 24, 1927; charge, state vagrancy.
As George Kelly, No. 2332, arrested Sheriff's Office, Tulsa, Oklahoma, January 12, 1928; charge, National Prohibition Act.
As George Kelley, No. 29962, received United States Penitentiary, Leavenworth, Kansas, February 11, 1928, from Tulsa, Oklahoma; crime, possession of liquor (Indian Cy); sentence 3 years.

George R. Kelly is wanted for the kidnaping of Charles F. Urschel at Oklahoma City, Oklahoma, on July 22, 1933.
Law enforcement agencies kindly transmit any additional information or criminal record to nearest office, Division of Investigation, U. S. Department of Justice.
If apprehended, please notify the Director, Division of Investigation, U. S. Department of Justice, Washington, D. C., or the Special Agent in Charge of the office of the Division of Investigation listed on the back hereof, which is nearest your city.

(over) Issued by: J. EDGAR HOOVER, Director.

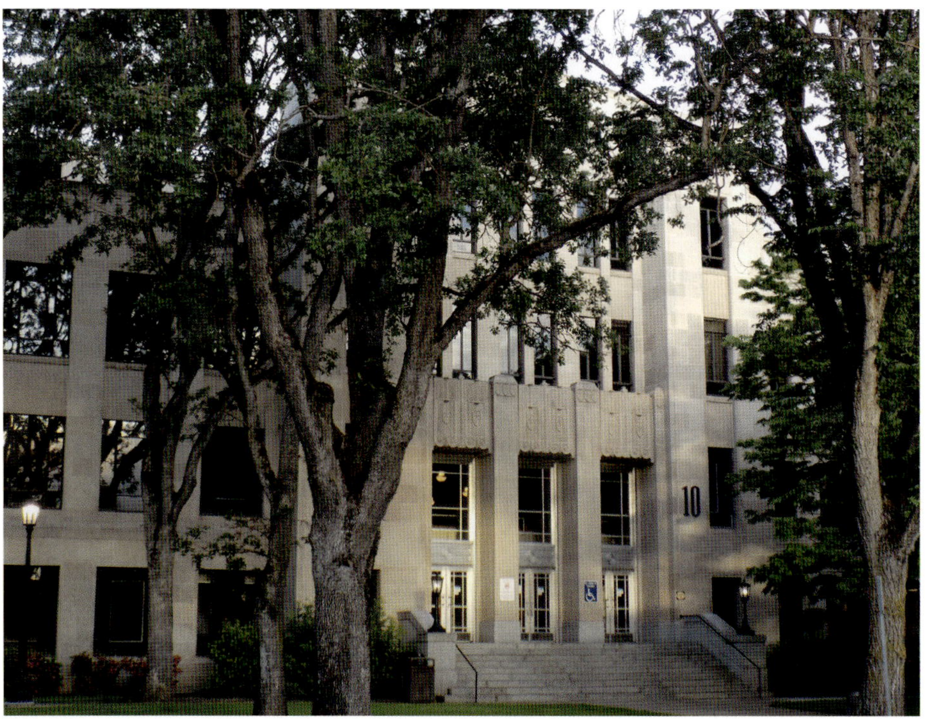

During the night of February 21, 1933, thieves broke into the Jackson County Courthouse and stole thousands of ballots. At the time of the theft, the recent election was being contested. The ballots were due to be re-counted the following morning. Most of the ballots were placed in bags, weighted down with rocks, and thrown into the Rogue River. Other ballots were burned.

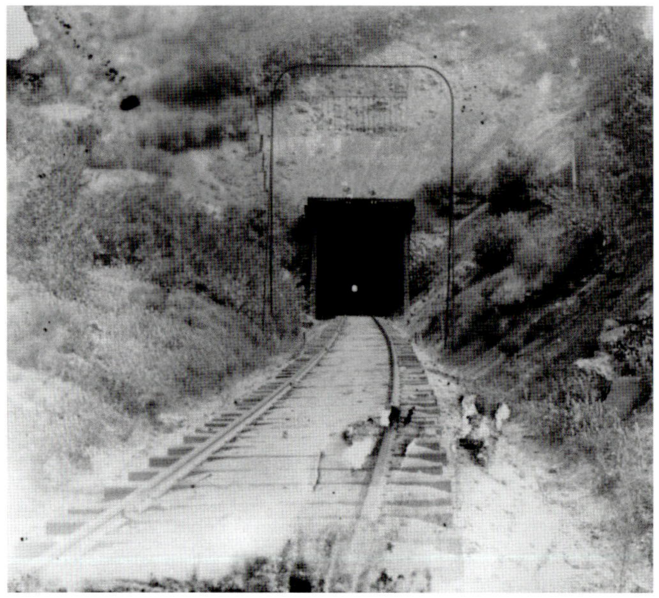

America's last great train robbery took place outside of Ashland on October 11, 1923. Four of the train's employees were killed when dynamite was used to access the mail car. The criminals believed that train 13, also known as the Gold Special, would be carrying a tremendous amount of money that they could easily grab and be set for life financially.

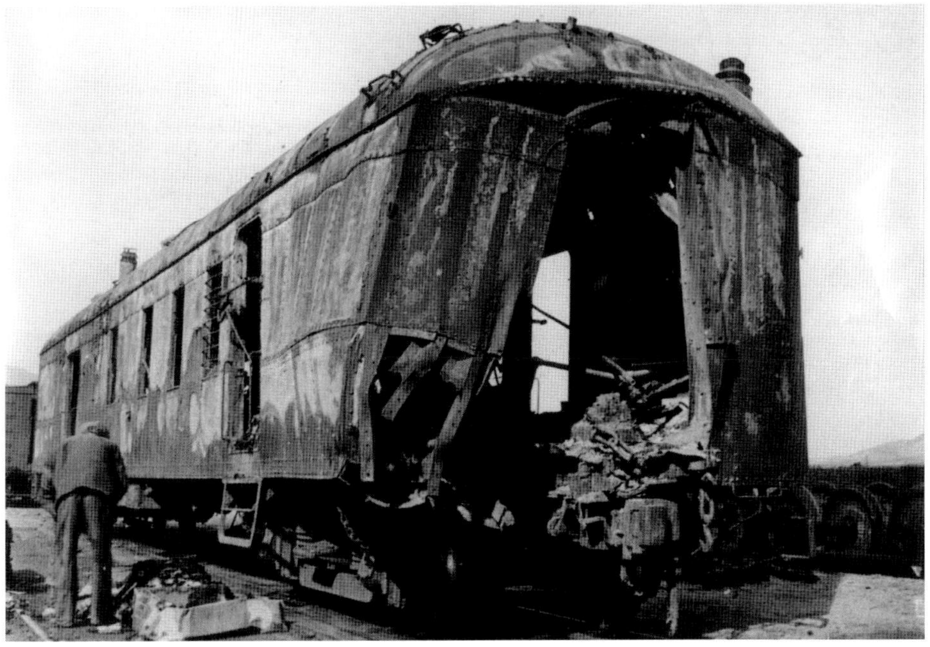

Within days, the authorities learned that the DeAutremont brothers, Ray, his twin brother, Roy, and younger brother, Hugh, were responsible for the crime.

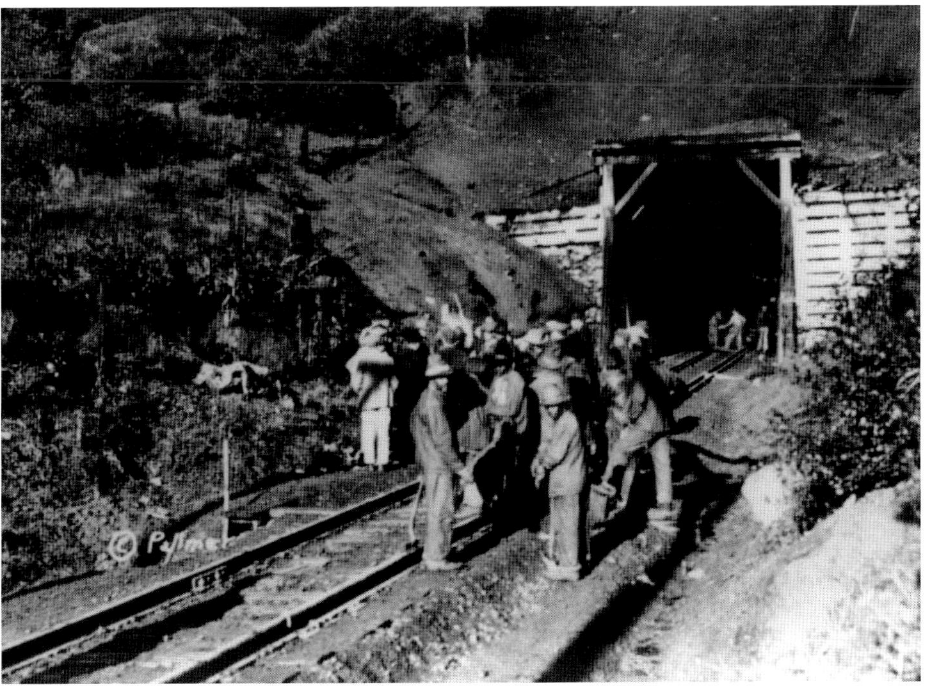

With wanted posters plastered all around the world, one would expect a quick arrest.

REWARD!

$14,400.00

Holdup of Southern Pacific Train No. 13, 1st Section, at Siskiyou, October 11, 1923

FOUR MEN KILLED

ward of $2500.00 will be paid by the Southern Pacific Railroad Company, of $300.00 by the American Rail-
press Company, and not to exceed $2,000.00 by the United States, for the arrest and conviction of each per-
)licated in the holdup.

least three persons participated in the crime. Below are photographs and descriptions of three brothers who
eved to have been connected with the holdup and who should be arrested on sight and held incommunicado.

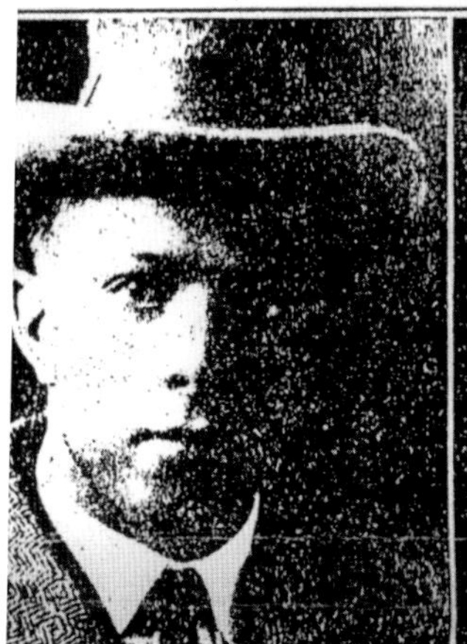
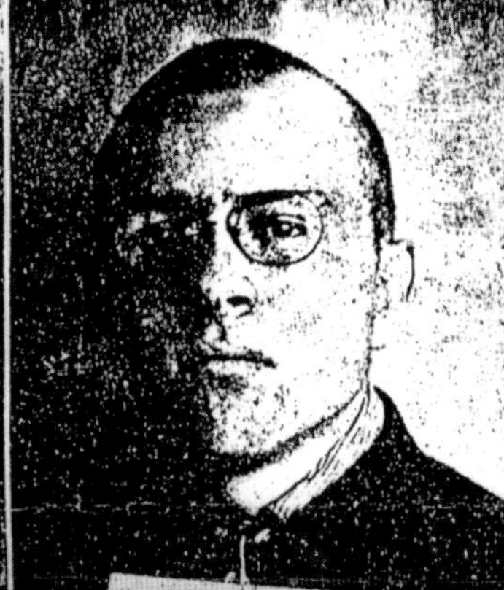
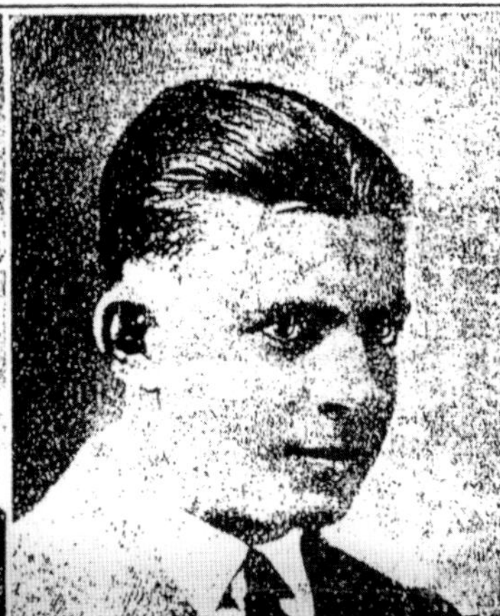

DESCRIPTIONS

Roy DeAutremont—Age 23 years;
t 135 to 140 lbs.; hair medium light
; height 5 feet 6 inches; complex-
nedium light; eyes light brown,
· small; wears nose eye glasses to
with; eyes appear somewhat granu-
and squinty; face broad, short cut
long nose and prominent nostrils.
smooth. No marks. Head round.

No. 2. Ray DeAutremont—Age 23 years;
height 5 feet 6 inches; weight 135 to 140
lbs.; complexion, medium light; hair,
medium light brown; broad face; prominent nostrils; short cut neck; face
smooth; eyes, light brown and small.
Eye tooth right side gold crown. Finger
Print Classification:

     31   1MM   14.
     28   0II   17.

Sentenced to one year Monroe, Washington, Reformatory, November 17th, 1919.
I. W. W. Organizer. Wears glasses when
reading.

No. 3. Hugh DeAutremont—Age 19, looks
older. Height 5 feet 7 inches; weight
135 lbs.; complexion fair; eyes blue
nose, slightly pug; hair medium light
slightly sandy and curly, bleached by
the sun; smooth shaven; wore short tes
rain coat; also had Mackinaw, but don'
know what color.

e above described men are twin brothers. It is most difficult for those not well
nted with them to tell them apart. The distinguishing features are that Ray probably
three or four pounds more and is a trifle taller than Roy. Ray is also slightly stooped
Ray is more given to talk and pleasantry than Roy, who is inclined to be quiet and
iming. They have both learned the barber trade and have worked in the woods as
s and it is probable that instead of being dressed up they may be dressed roughly and
gers.

All three men are loggers and may be found in logging camps working as choker setters, hook tenders or whis
nks. They have spoken of taking a long sea voyage and look-out should be kept for them attempting to ship a
orts. They speak Spanish fluently and may attempt to cross the Mexican border. Formerly lived at Lakewood

In the end, it took almost four years and a half-million dollars to locate the DeAutremont brothers in what
became known at the time as "the world's largest manhunt."

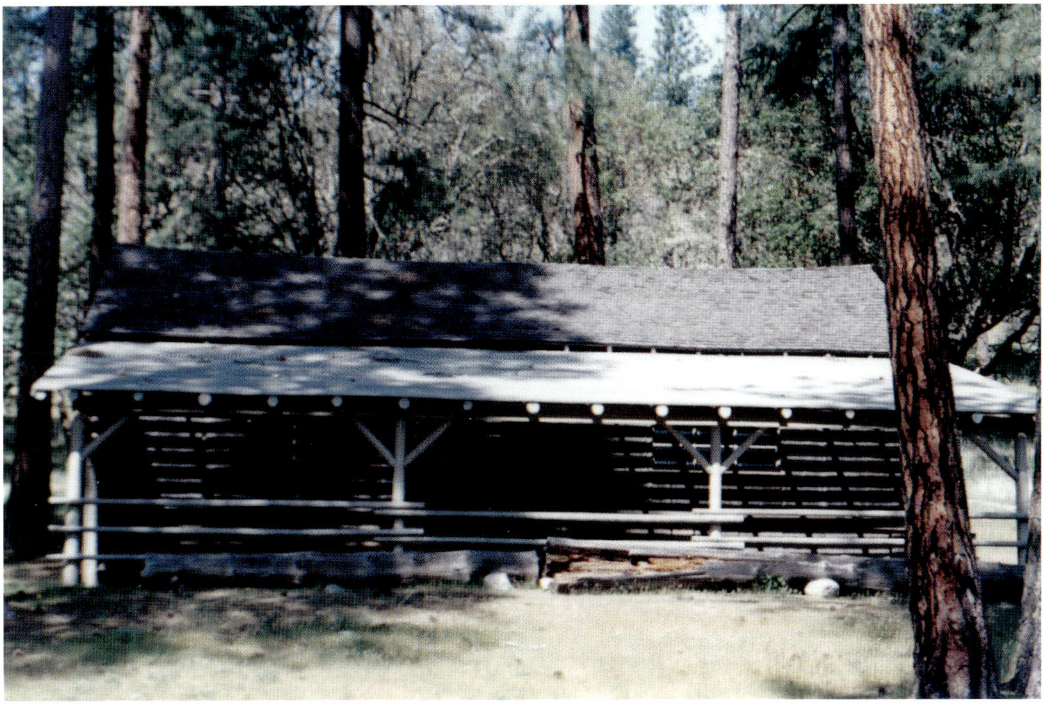

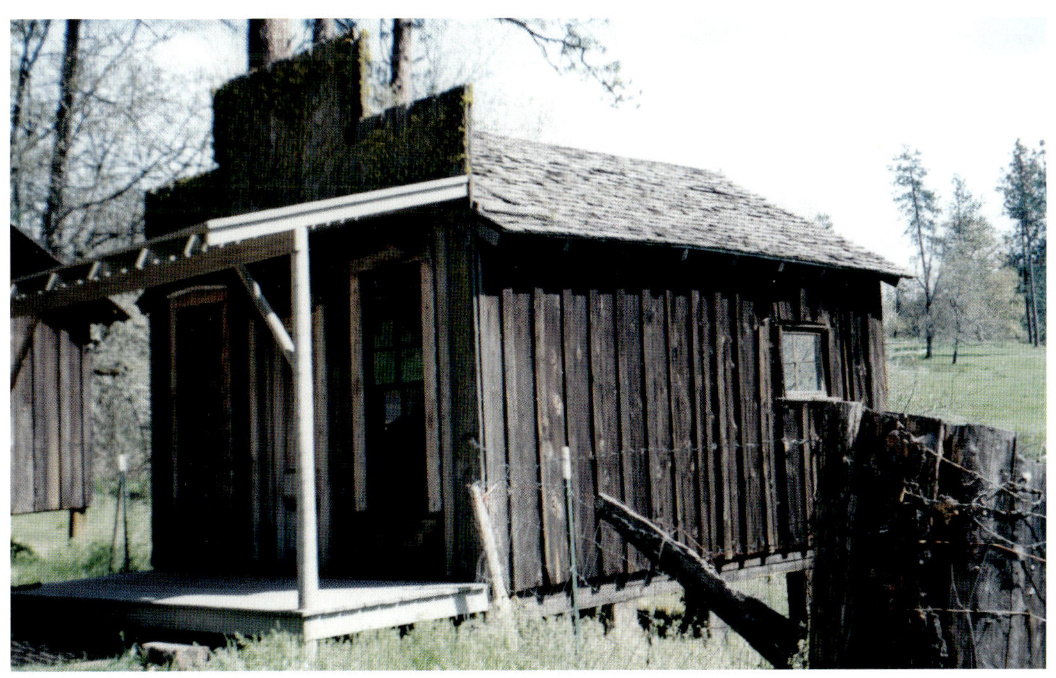

The ghost town of Buncom stands today to show what a mining camp from the late 1800s looked like.

The original post office, bunkhouse, and the cookhouse remain.

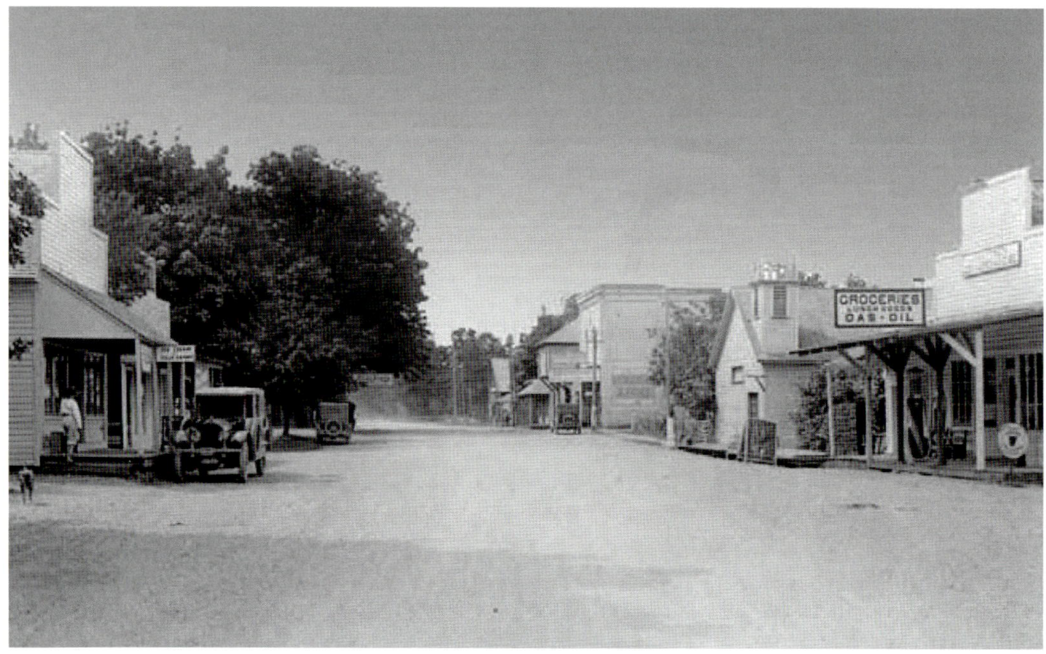

For a short period of time in the late 1850s, the town of Kerby was named "Napoleon." The locals thought that Josephine should have a Napoleon, but the name was short lived.

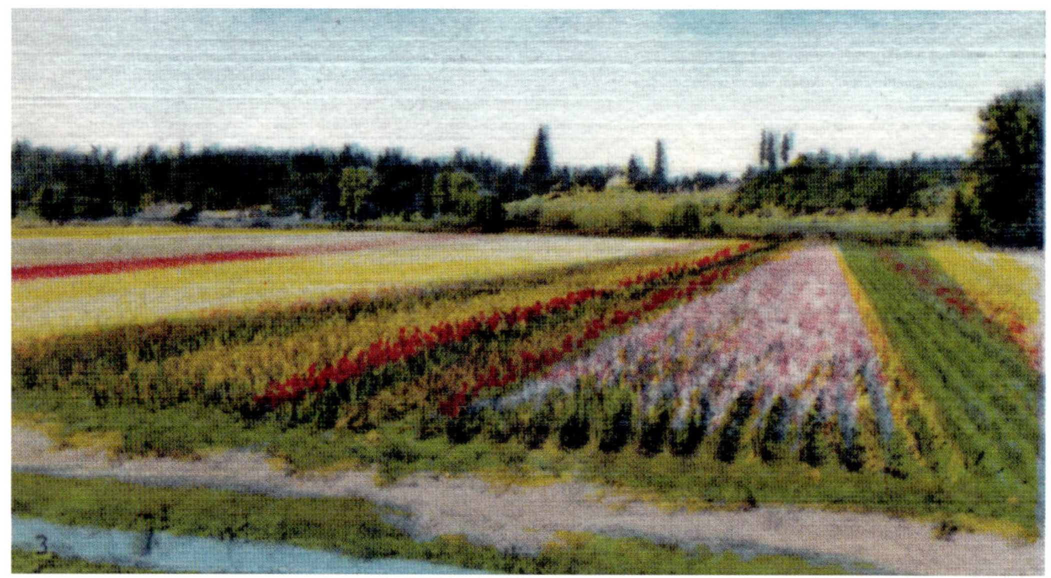

Grants Pass used to be well known for their gladiolus flower bulbs. In 1927, there were forty-three acres planted in gladiolus bulbs. That increased until they reached a peak of 1,500 acres of gladiolus bulbs. Festivals were held every year to celebrate the flowers. After the child actress, Shirley Temple, visited Grants Pass, a gladiolus bulb was named for her.

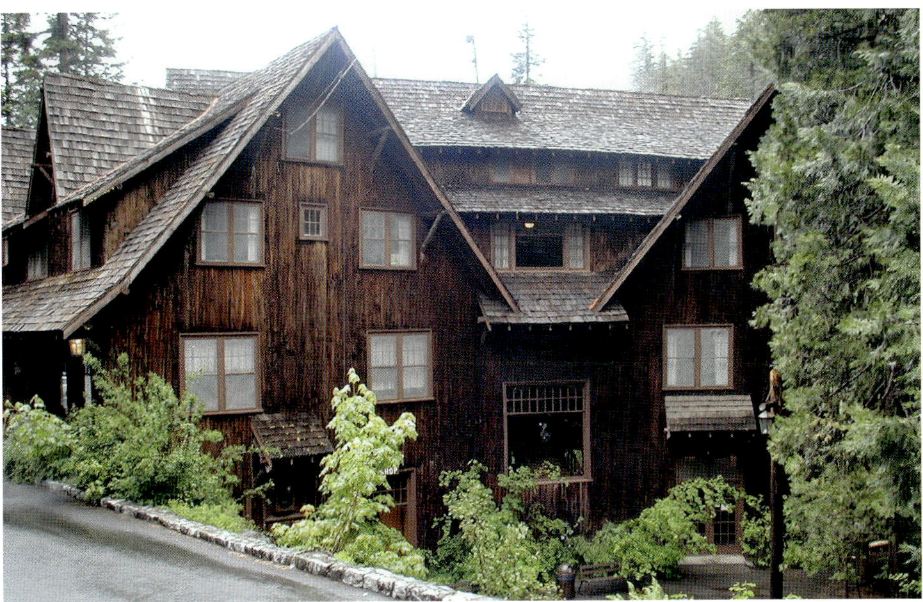

Elijah Davidson is credited with being the first person to discover the Oregon Caves. He came across them while bear hunting with his dog Bruno. Early visitors took a dirt road and then had to hike six miles to the caves. Pack animals could be rented for $3.50 for a round trip. In 1909 President Taft established the Oregon Caves as a National Monument.

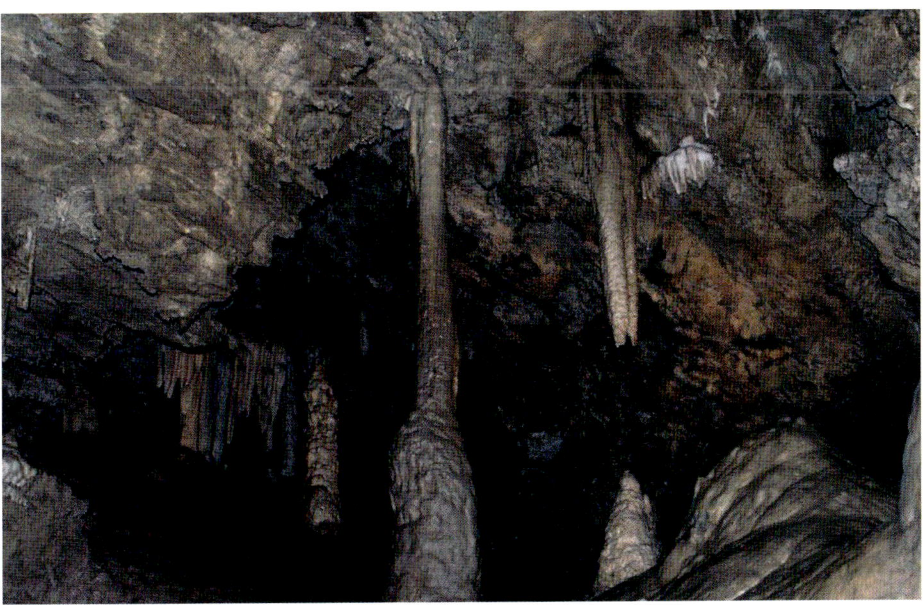

Early on, there were no accommodations for meals or lodging. The U.S. Forest Service warned, "Visitors planning to go through the caves should provide themselves with candles and overalls or old clothes. Ladies should wear overalls, riding trousers, or old trousers of some sort. Heavy, hob-nailed shoes will also be of assistance in climbing about in the caves."

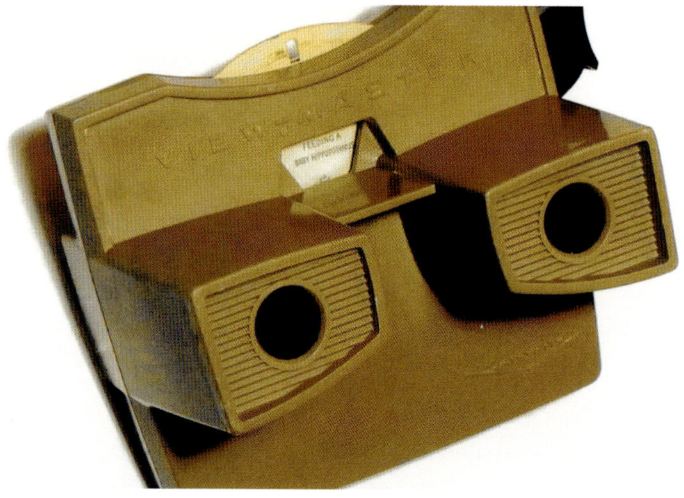

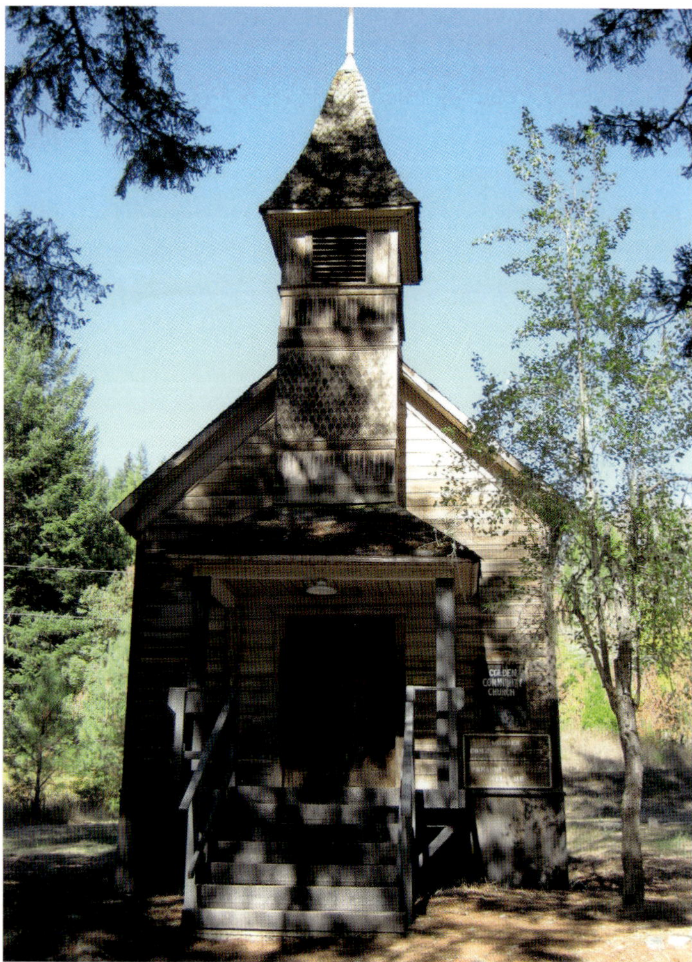

Above: A chance meeting at the Oregon Caves National Monument in 1938 led to the invention of the View-Master. William Gruber met Harold Graves, who owned an Oregon postcard manufacturing business. Gruber showed Graves his invention: two Kodak Bantam cameras mounted together on an aluminum tripod. Gruber also invented a way to mount tiny pieces of color transparency film into tiny reels made of heavy cardstock. They put their businesses together and thus the View-Master was created.

Left: What began as a mining camp morphed into the town of Golden. But when the last of the gold was gone, people moved on, seeking other opportunities. The ghost town of Golden consists of a church, a former residence, a shed, and the town's post office and store.

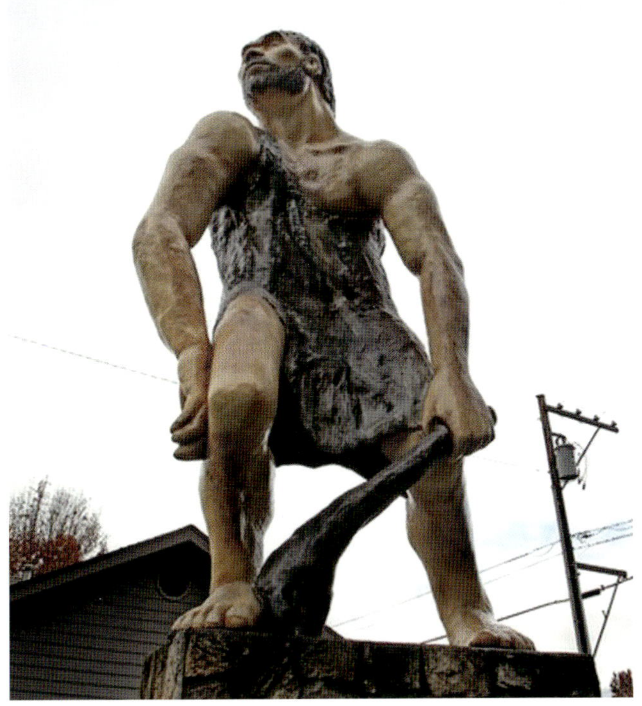

Right: Grants Pass Cavemen began in 1922 as a way to boost tourism. A group of men would dress up in animal skins and carry clubs. They promoted the Oregon Caves National Monument and the Redwood Highway.

Below: The slogan that made Grants Pass famous: It's The Climate. John Hampshire Sr. is credited with coming up with the slogan in 1917. He was a member of the Grants Pass Commercial Club and worked tirelessly to promote Grants Pass using the slogan. Over the years, the signs have changed, but the slogan has endured.

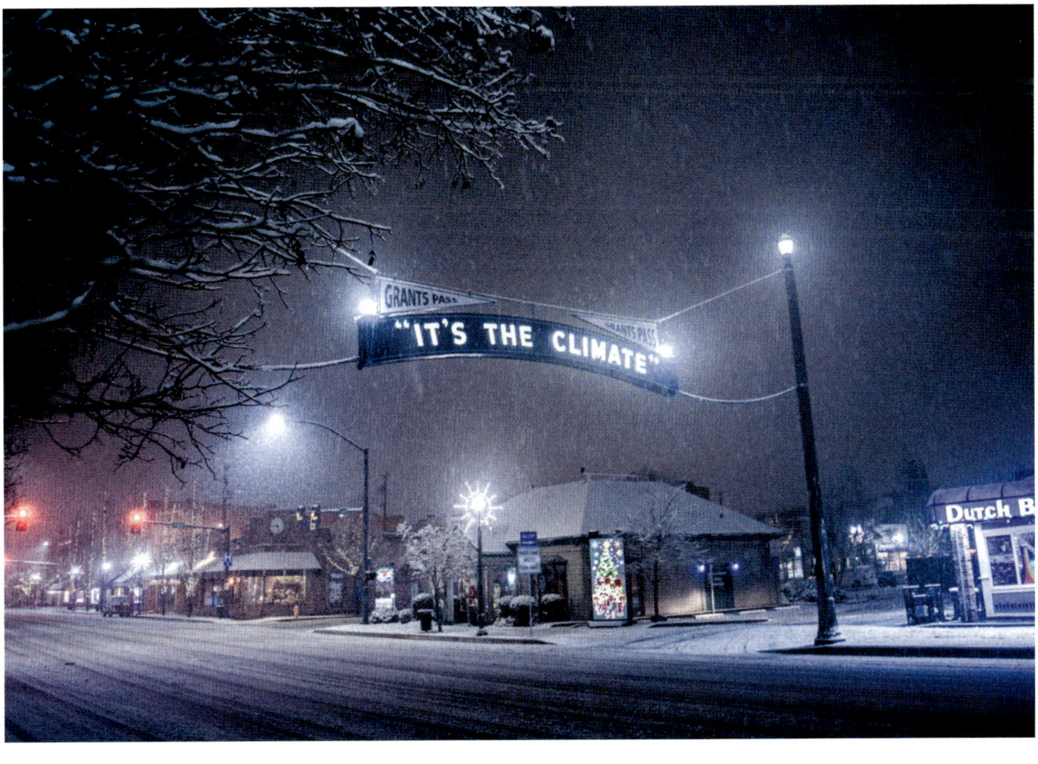

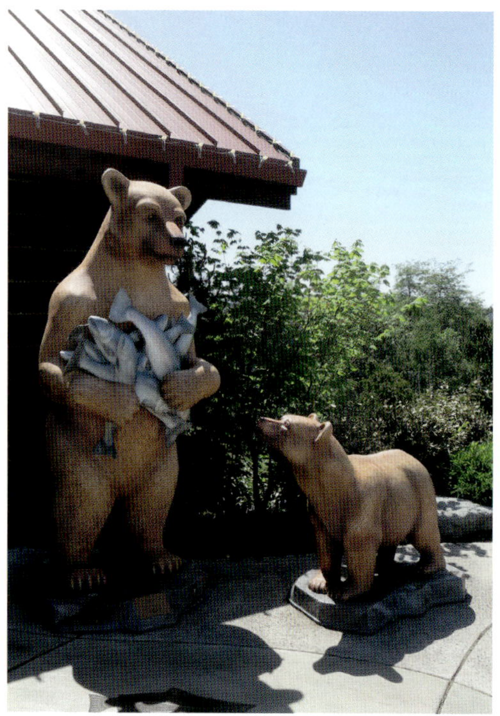

Left: For many years, the city of Grants Pass has been overrun with gigantic bears. The fiberglass bears are designed by artists. They are placed throughout the downtown area and auctioned off to raise money for local causes.

Below: Wildlife Images has been rehabilitating sick, injured, and orphaned animals since 1981. The twenty-four-acre park is home to numerous animals who act as ambassadors for the public who visit. The center provides educational programs on wildlife, conservation, and the environment.

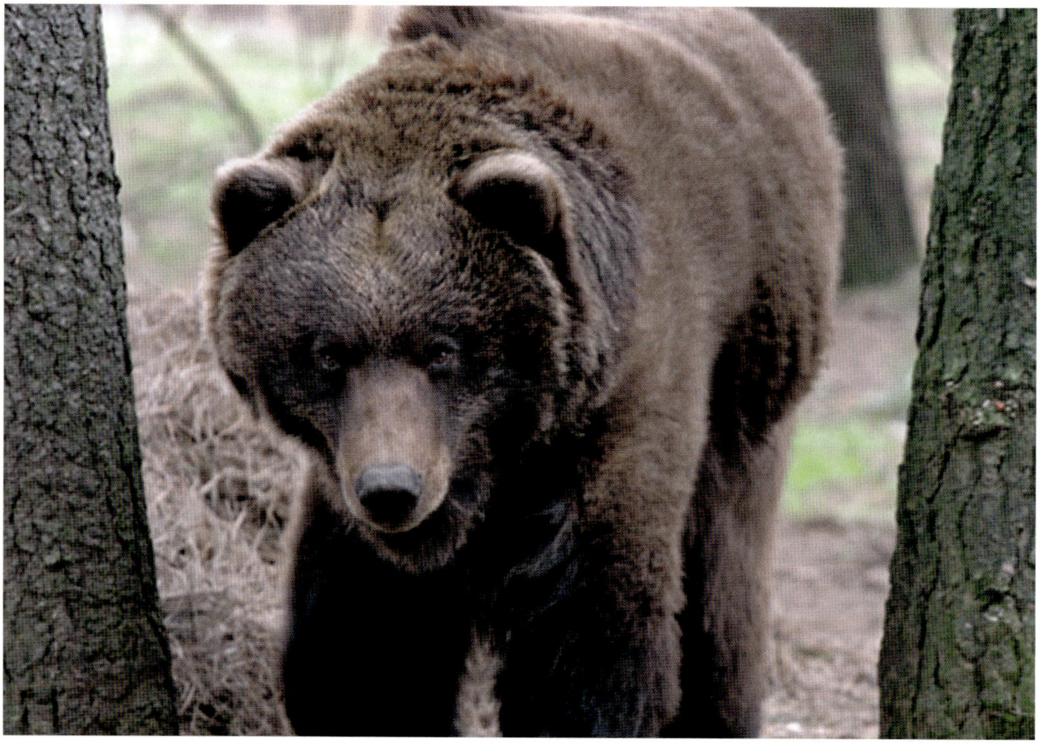

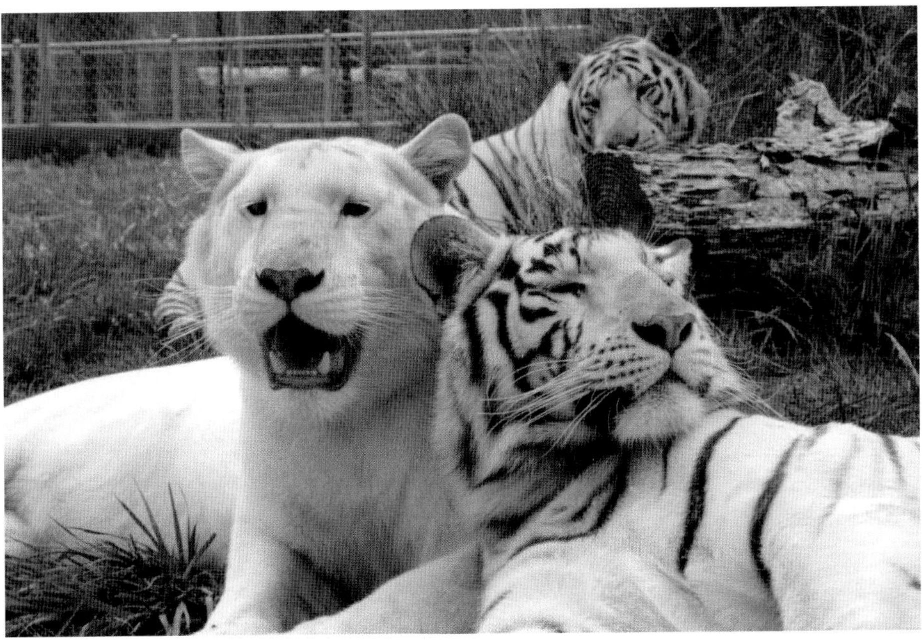

Cave Junction is home to the Great Cats World Park. Pictured are Sugar, Spice, and Scooby.

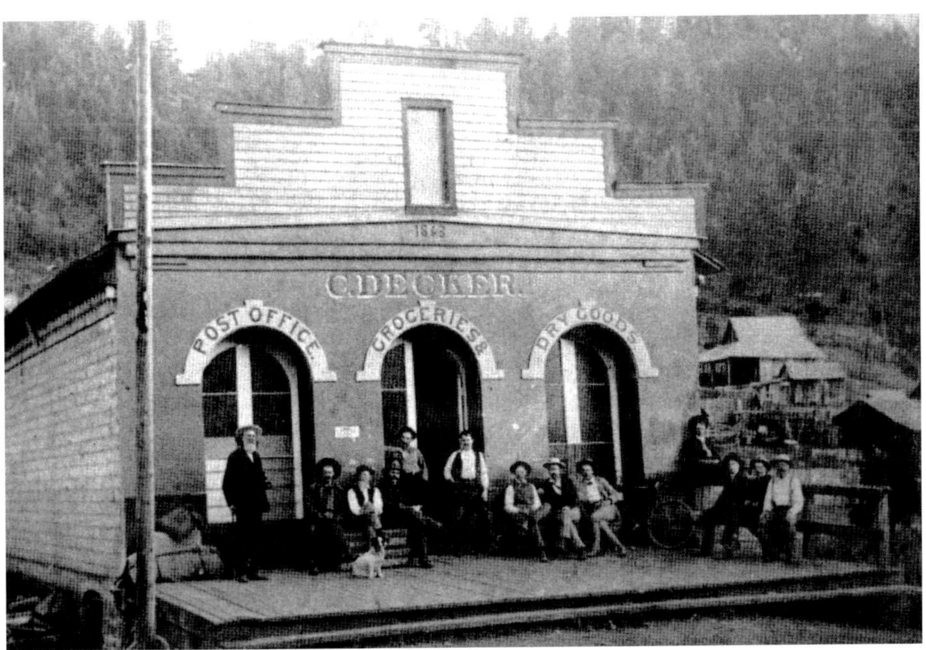

Where is Waldo? For Josephine County, the answer lies on Highway 199 near the present-day town of O'Brien. In the 1850s the town of Waldo was an active mining community complete with houses, a cobbler shop, a bowling alley, blacksmith shops, a butcher shop, a brewery, many stores, hotels, and saloons. By the 1920s, the gold was gone, and the town began to fade into history.

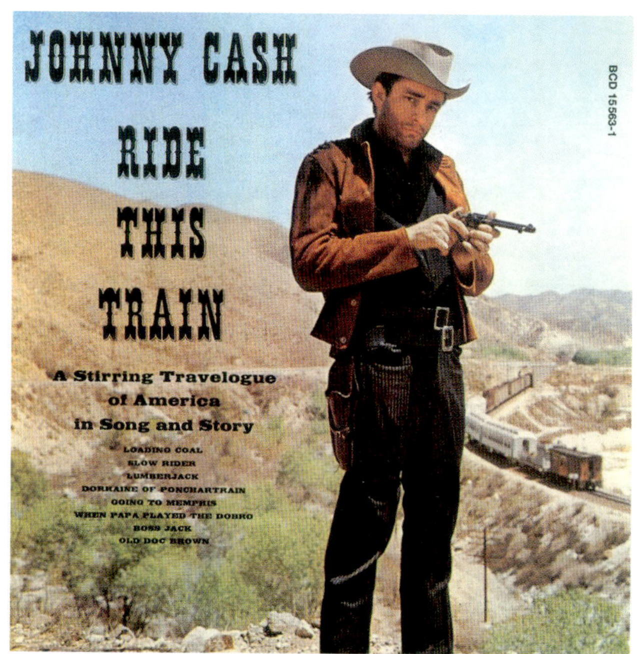

In 1960, Johnny Cash released his song, Lumberjack, after spending time in Oregon. In the song he reminisces about his time working as a lumberjack. In part the lyrics are, "Ride this train to Roseburg, Oregon. Now there's a town for you. And you talk about rough. You know a lot of places in the country claim Paul Bunyon lived there. But you should have seen Roseburg when me and my daddy come there."

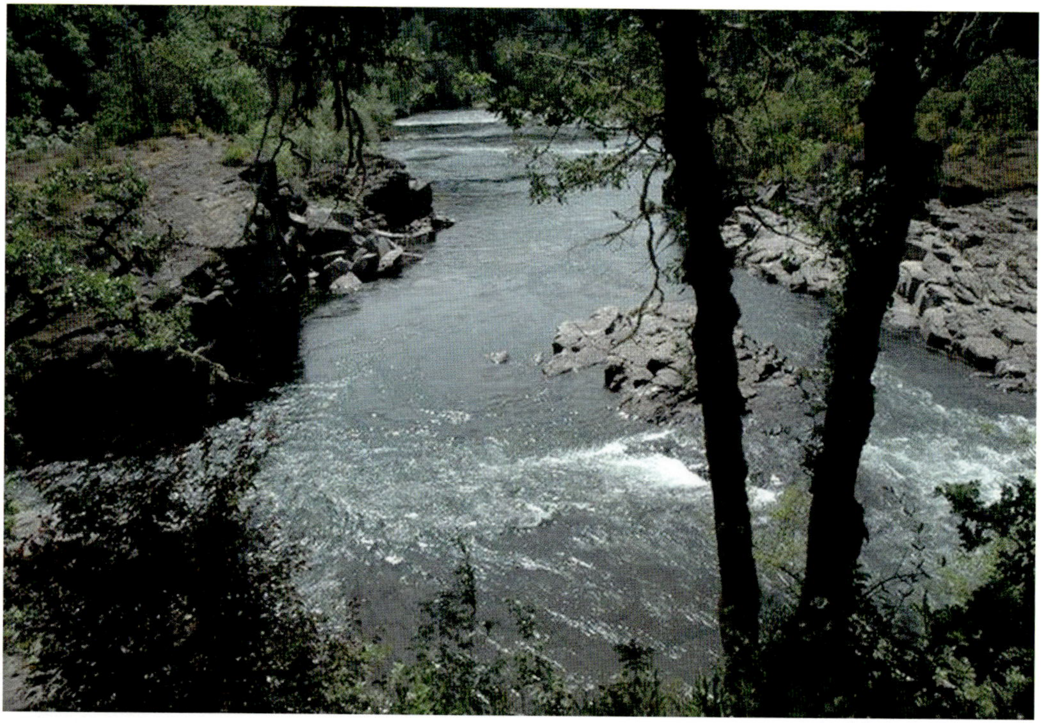

The Colliding Rivers got its name because the Little River in Glide collides almost head-on with the North Umpqua River. It is the only place in Oregon where a river meets its tributary at a straight angle.

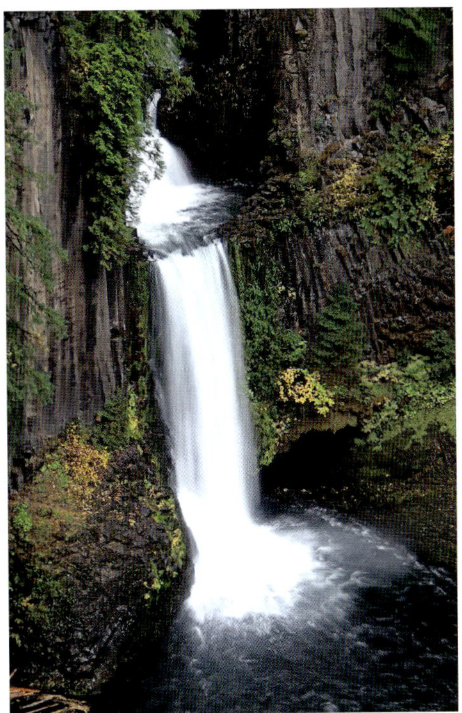

Right: The stretch of Highway 138 between Roseburg and Diamond Lake is known as the Highway of Waterfalls.

Below: When people in Roseburg went to bed on the night of August 6, 1959, they had no way of knowing that the next day the town of Roseburg would be covered in nearly every major newspaper in America as well as in *Time* magazine and *Life* magazine.

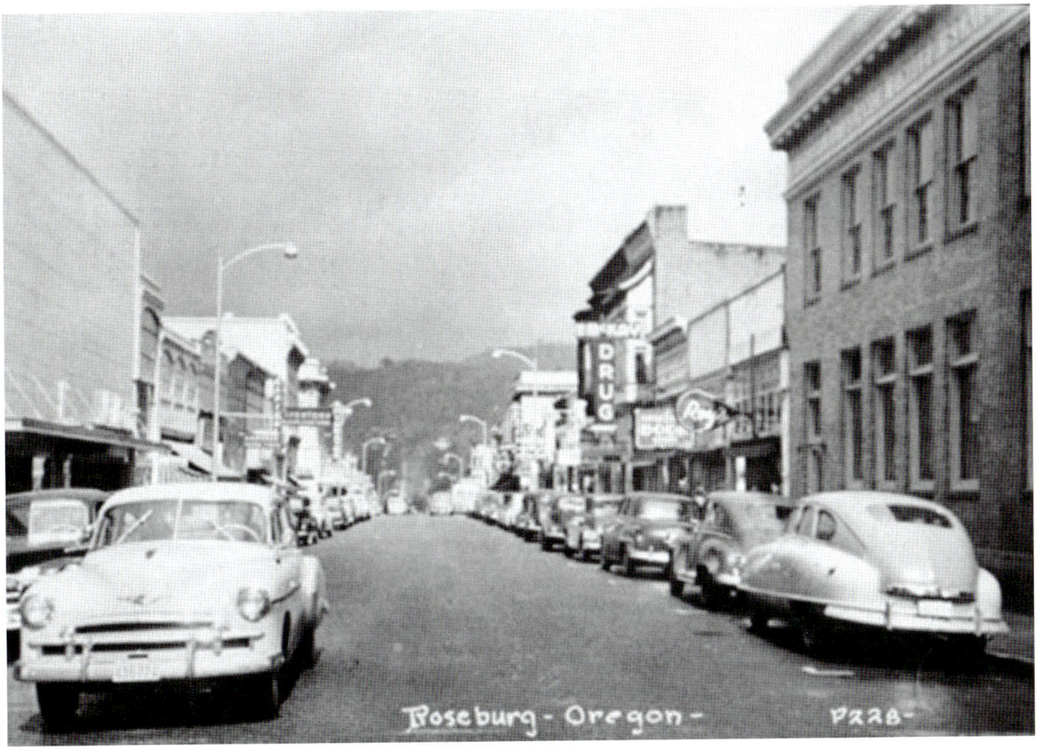

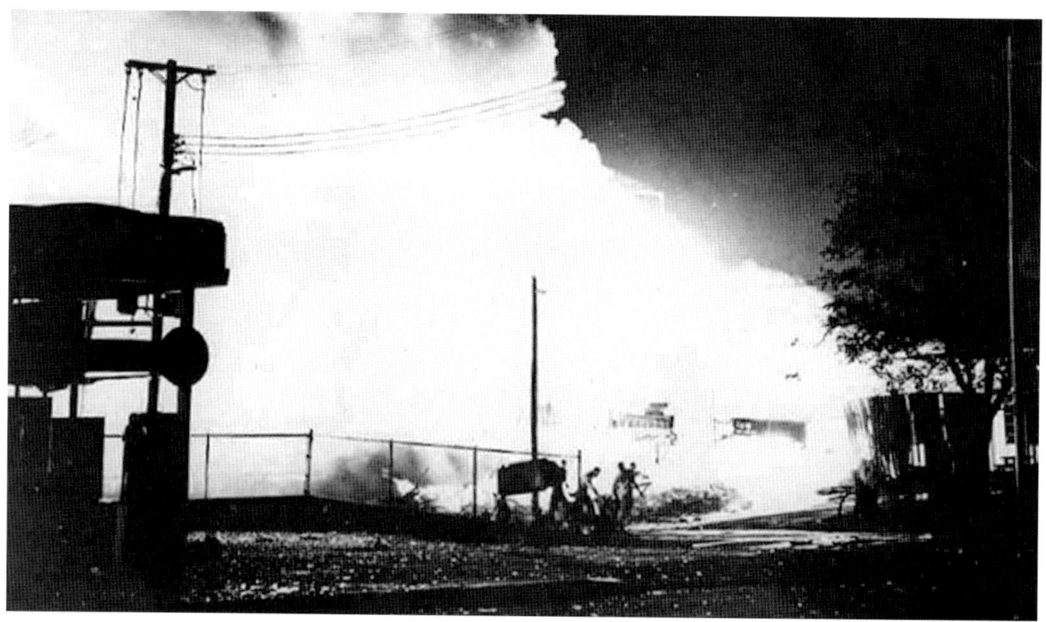

On the evening of August 6, 1959, a truck driver for Pacific Powder Company out of Seattle, Washington, finished his shift driving on the highway and stopped in Roseburg for the night. He ate dinner and then checked into a motel for the night. During the night, a fire broke out at the Gerretson Building Supply Company.

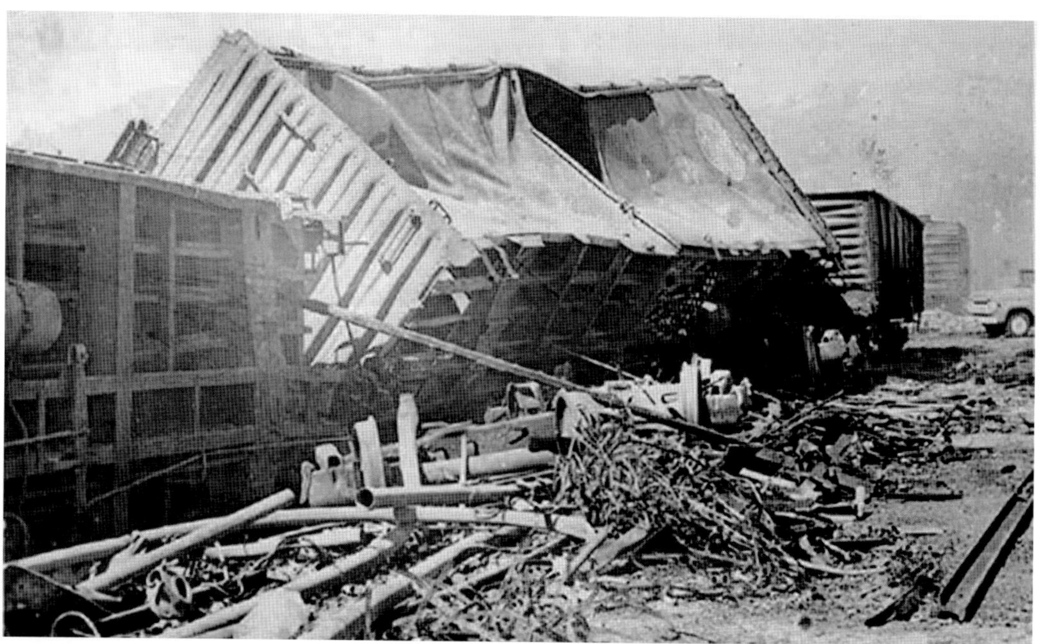

The Pacific Powder Company truck was loaded with four tons of solid ammonium nitrate fertilizer and two tons of dynamite. The truck caught fire and within minutes the explosion leveled downtown Roseburg.

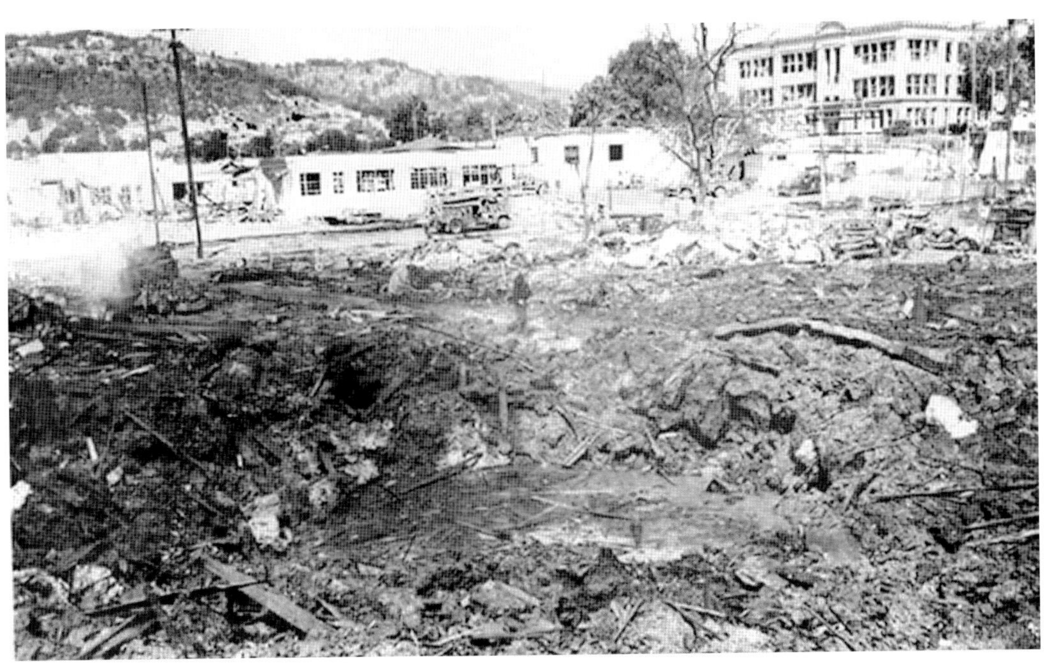

The explosion tore a hole fifty feet across and fifteen feet deep where the truck had been parked. Water mains burst and filled the crater left by the explosion. Windows in homes and businesses were broken within miles of the downtown area.

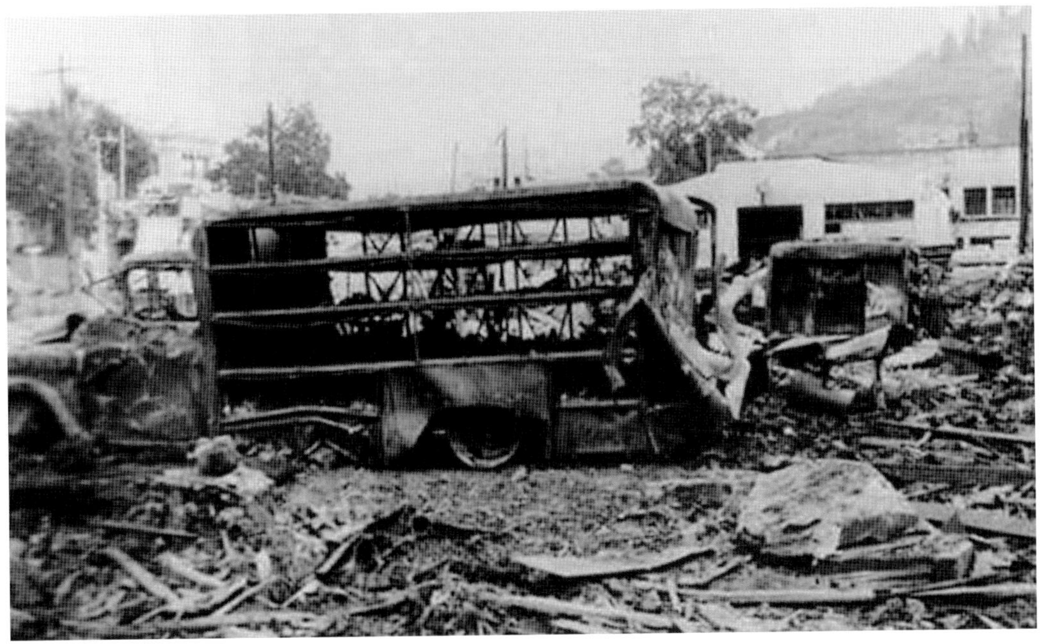

Firefighters came from as far as Eugene and Springfield to help. Firefighter Lyle Wescott told the reporters, "I looked down and saw the skin peeling off my hand."

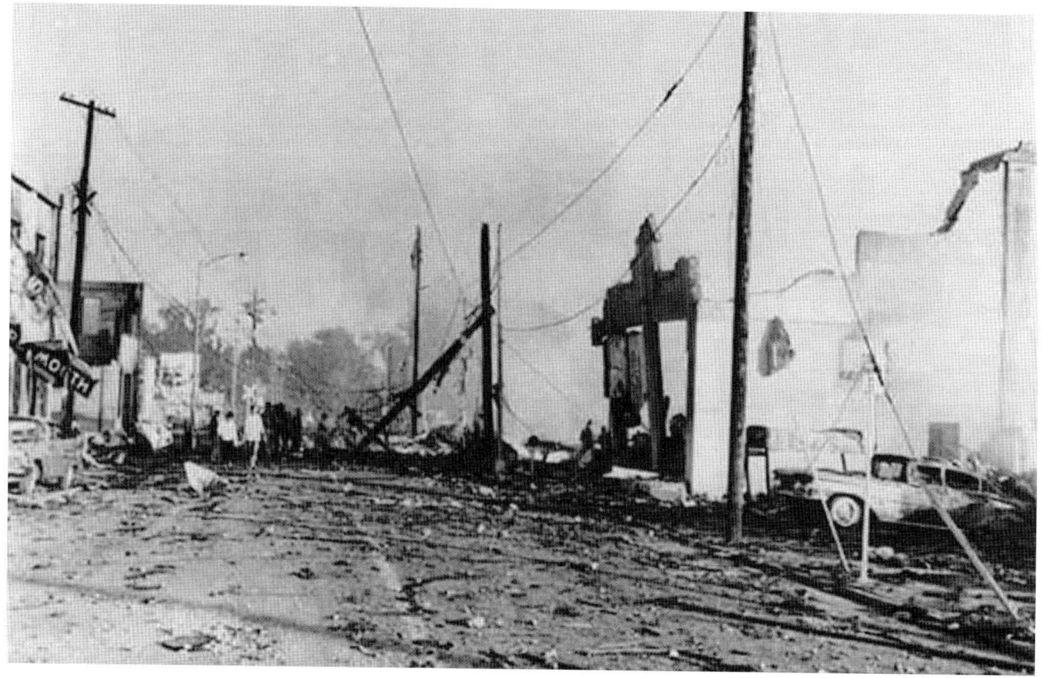

Embers from the blast started smaller fires in the area. By early morning, all the fires were out. The National Guard was deployed to guard against looting. The local police and sheriff assisted.

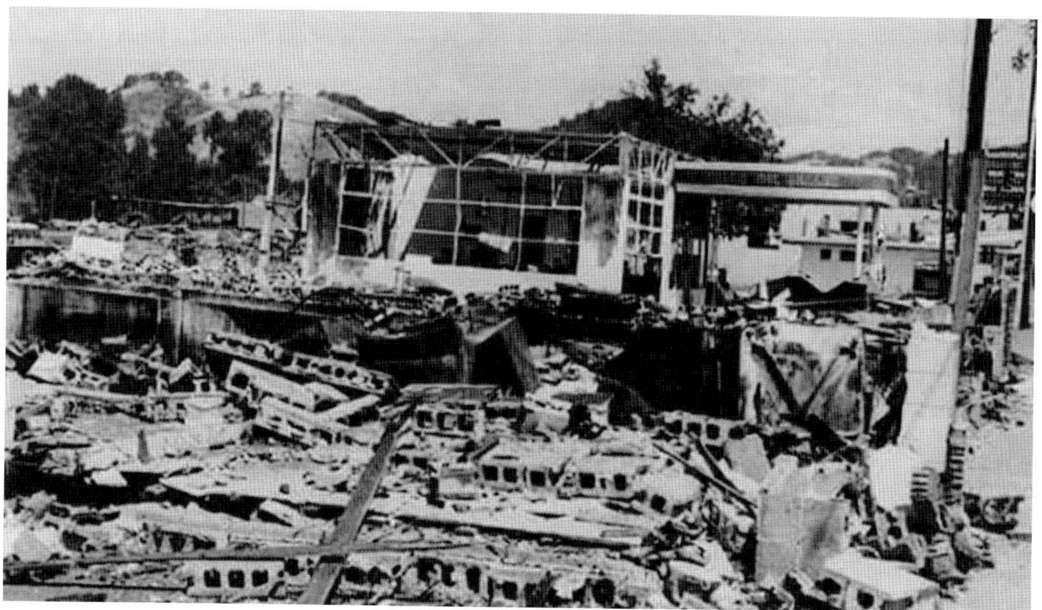

The explosion and fire became known as the "Roseburg Blast." Businesses, homes, apartments, and boarding houses were destroyed in the immediate area. The damage stretched for many blocks and rendered homes, businesses, apartments, and a school unstable.

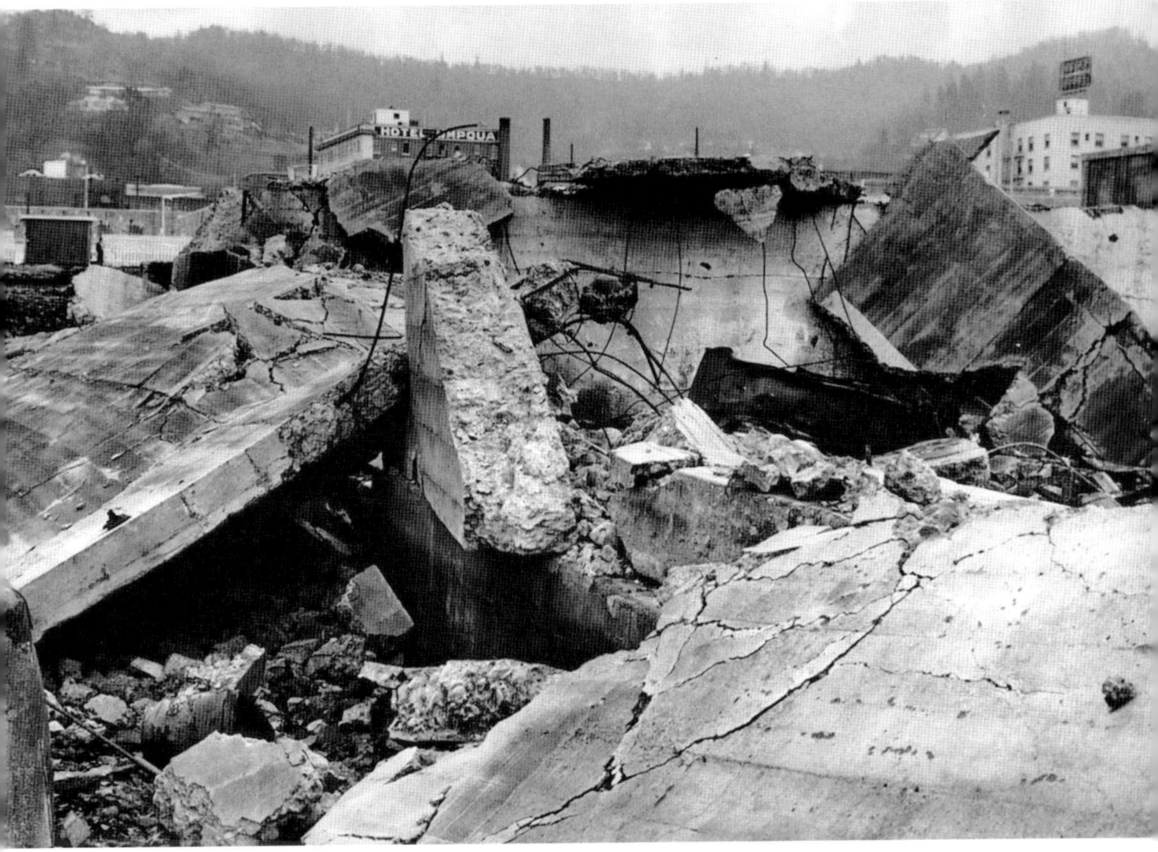

Above: Fourteen people died and more than 100 were injured in the Roseburg Blast. The Roseburg Blast was a catalyst for enacting laws regarding transporting explosives. It was also used as an example for cities across America to be prepared for a disaster.

Right: Alvin Buckelew was born in 1927. He became a child actor. [*Photo courtesy of Harold Burris*]

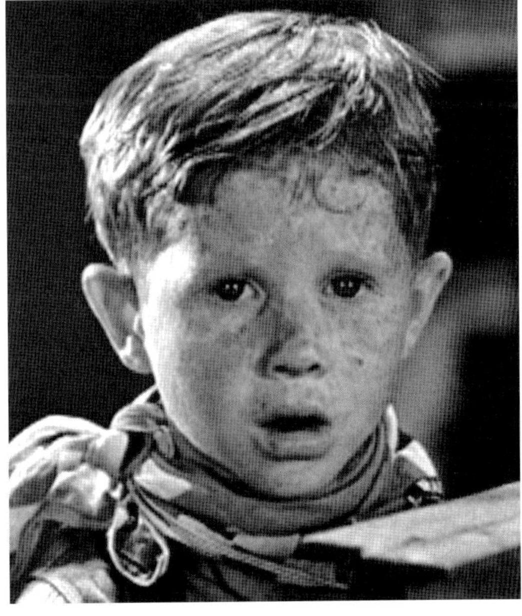

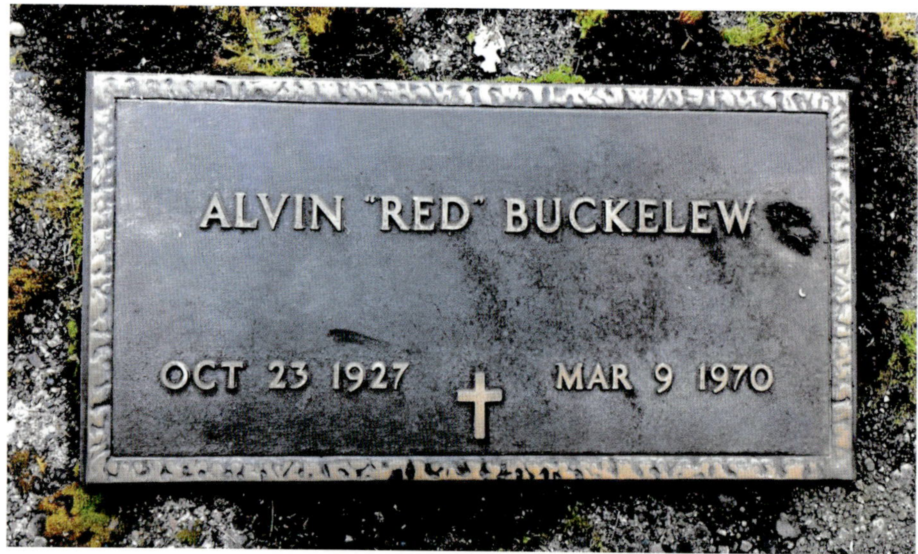

At the age of seven, Alvin began acting in the *Our Gangs* short films and *The Little Rascals*. The films were based on real life experiences portrayed by children who were not trained actors. Alvin is buried in the cemetery in Drain. [*Photo courtesy of Harold Burris*]

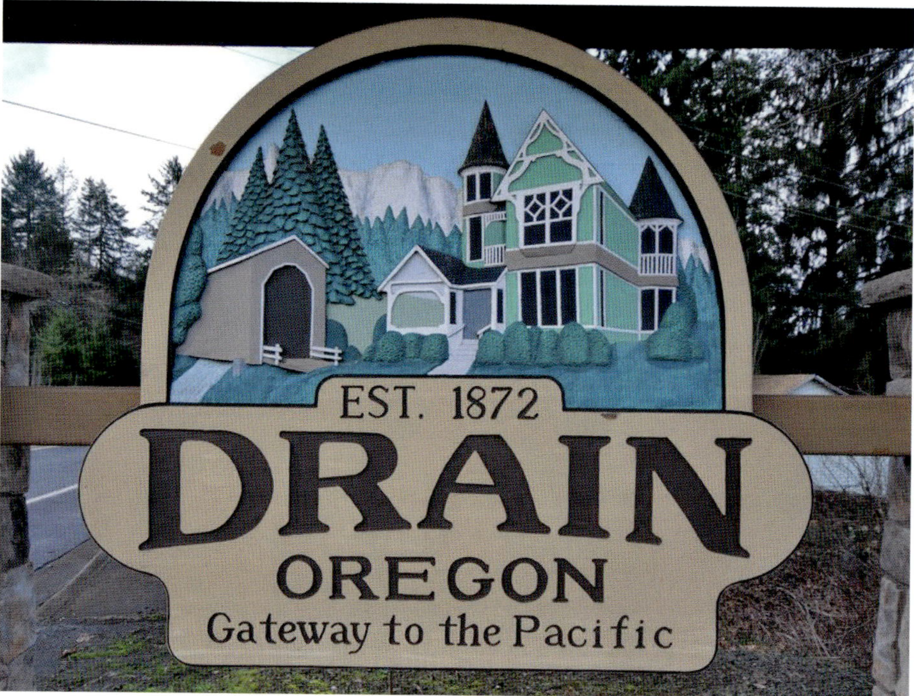

The town of Drain is named for pioneer Charles Drain. He purchased some property in 1861. In 1872, when the railroad was being built, it reached Douglas County. Charles and his son, John, sold sixty acres of their land to the Oregon and California Railroad Company for one dollar in order to create a town.

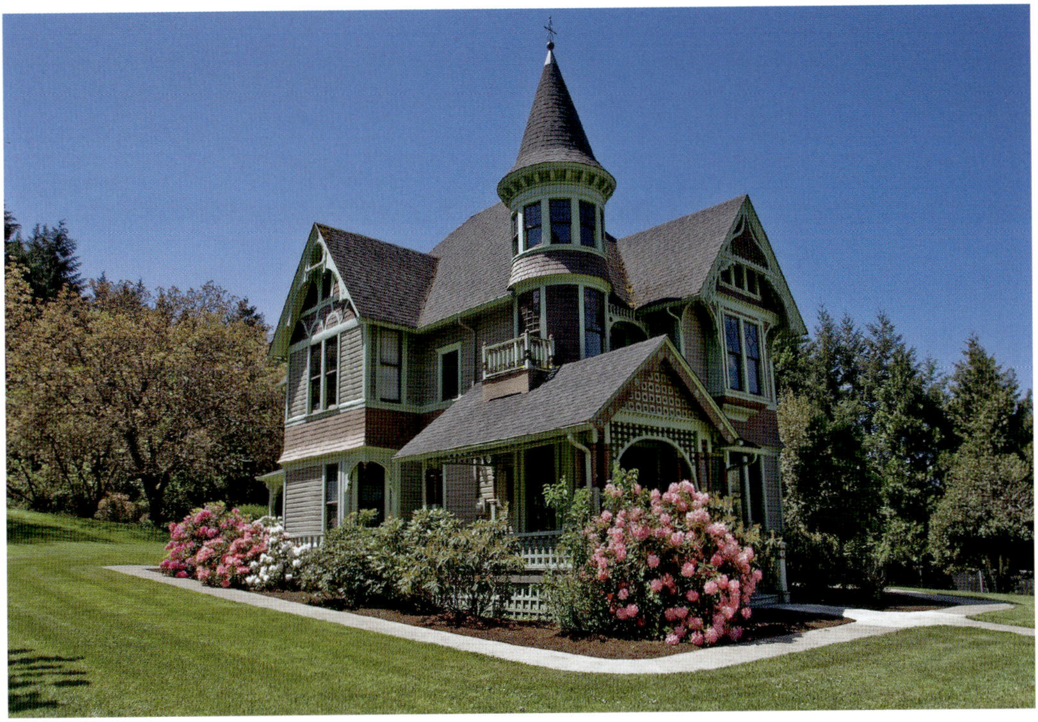

Above: Charles Drain's youngest son, Charles, and his wife, Anna, moved into this beautiful Queen Anne house in 1895. The house is listed on the National Register of Historic Places. [*Photo courtesy of Harold Burris*]

Right: In 1959, the Drain Chamber of Commerce sponsored an Oregon Trail reenactment. The wagon master was former President Harry S. Truman. [*Photo courtesy of Harold Burris*]

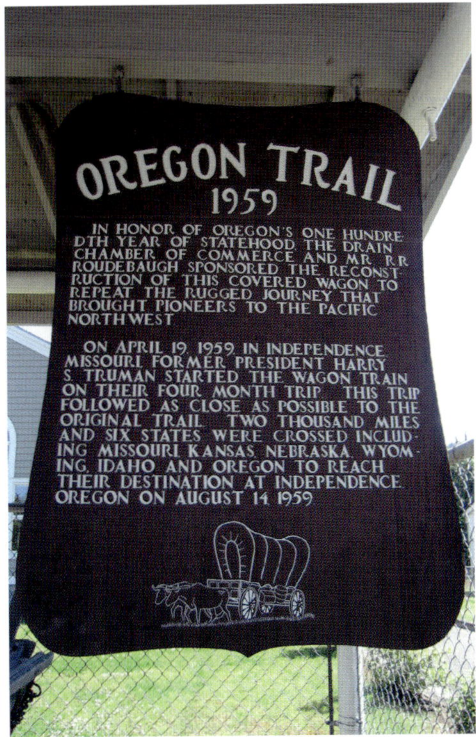

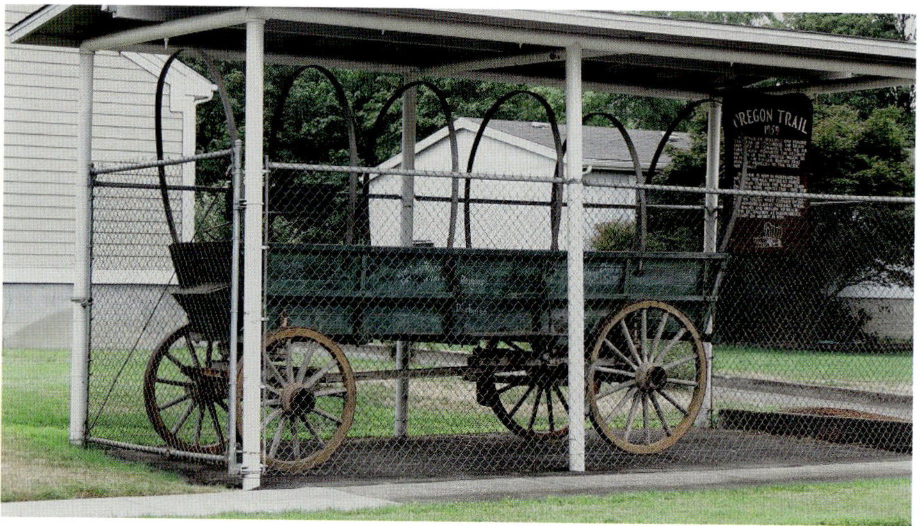

The wagon left from the same place that the original pioneers left from: Independence, Missouri. They crossed through six states, Missouri, Kansas, Nebraska, Wyoming, Idaho, and Oregon. After four months and two thousand miles, they arrived in Oregon on August 14, 1959. [*Photo courtesy of Harold Burris*]

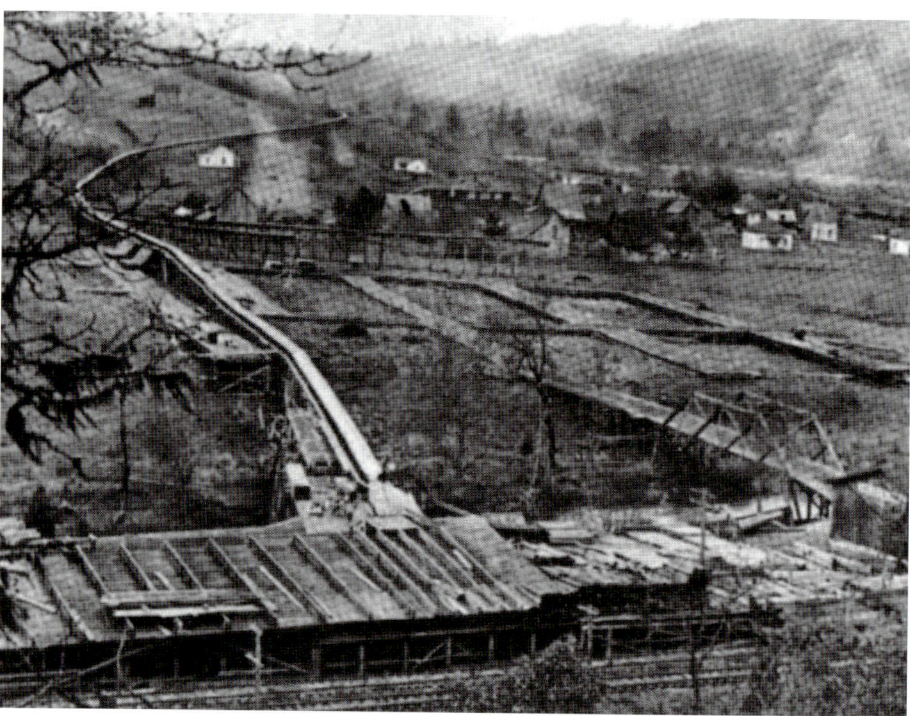

The Skelley Lumber Company built a flume in 1904-1906 to transport logs from the forest to a nearby mill near Drain. The flume was a V-shaped trough that was filled with water from a source near the mill. The length of the flume was 5.25 miles. It took 1,500,000 feet of lumber to build the flume. Employees known as "flume herders" kept the logs going in the correct direction. The company shut down in 1911. [*Photo courtesy of Harold Burris*]

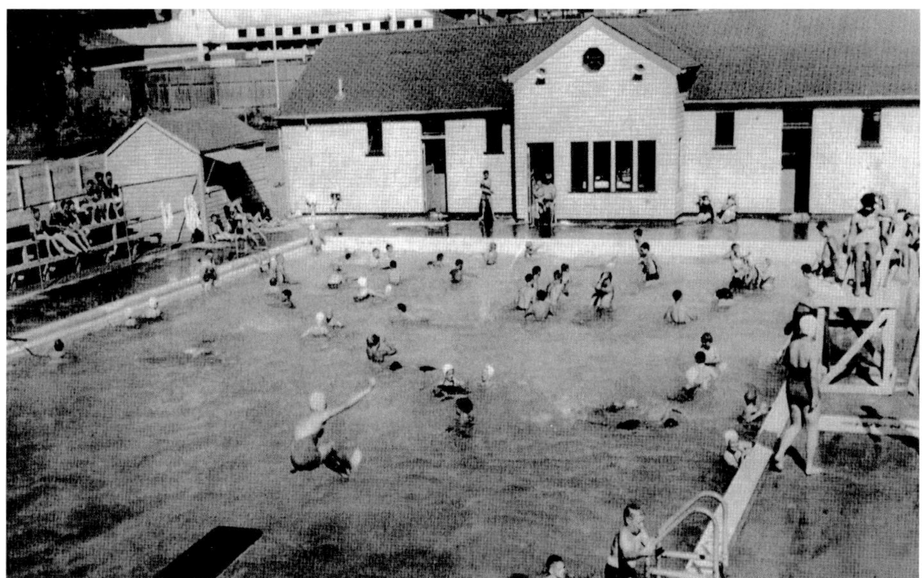

In 1948, the North Douglas Living War Memorial was dedicated. It took five years, but the small town of Drain, population 1,000, raised $100,000 to build the war memorial. The North Douglas Living War Memorial included the swimming pool pictured, tennis courts, and a lighted baseball diamond. They did not borrow any money, but instead raised the money through scrap drives, benefit shows, and auctions. Local businesses donated some of the labor and materials. [*Photo courtesy of Harold Burris*]

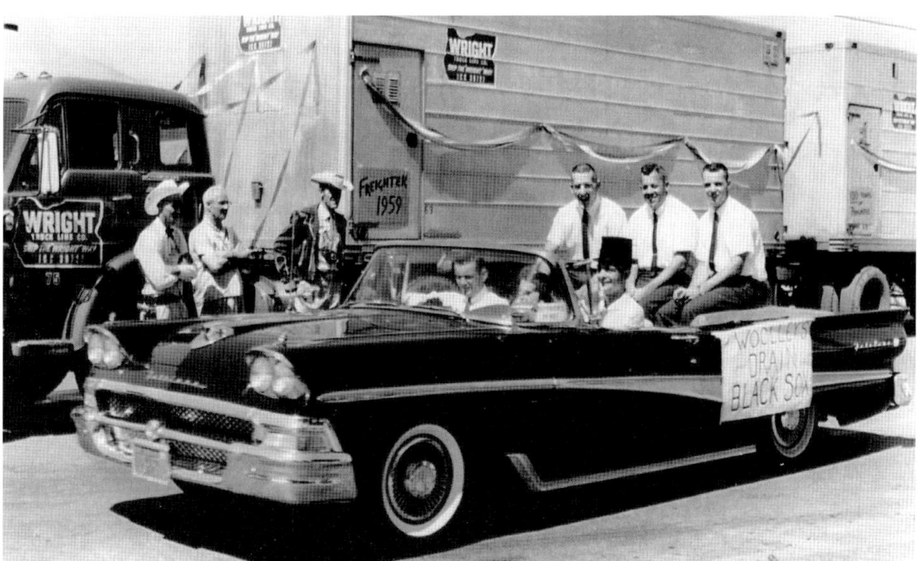

In 1958, the Drain Black Sox baseball team was sponsored by Woolley Lumber Company. The team was the first sponsored team from the West Coast to win the National Baseball Congress Tournament. The tournament was held in Wichita, Kansas. Player Jim Pifher told reporters that the other team was making fun of the name, Drain. He recalled they weren't laughing when Drain won. The team was later inducted into the Oregon Sports Hall. [*Photo courtesy of Harold Burris*]

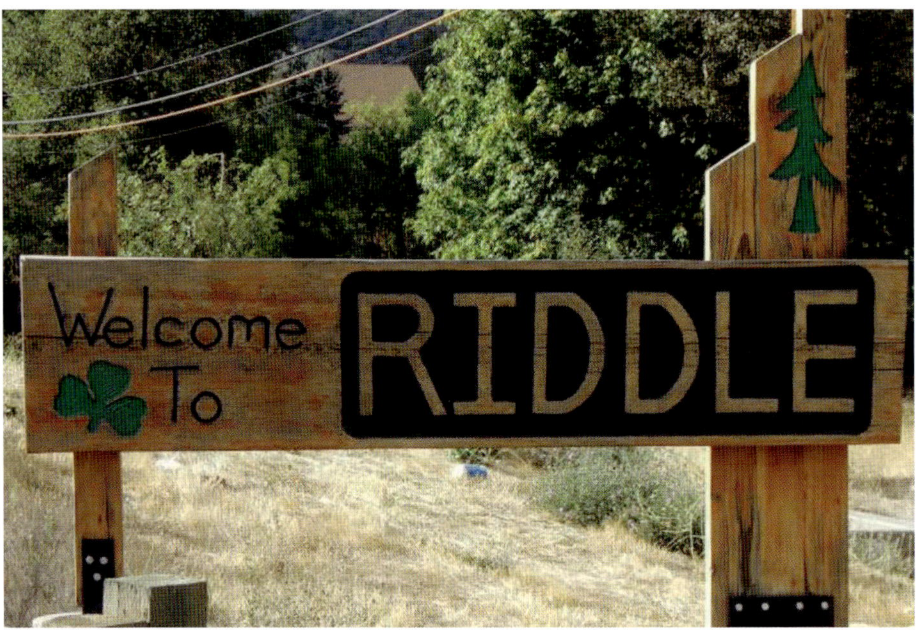

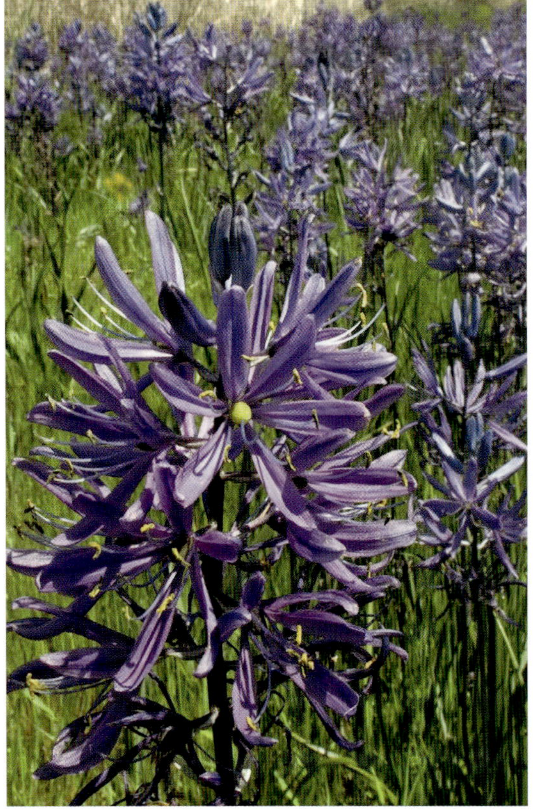

Above: The town of Riddle was named after William H. Riddle. He came overland from Springfield, Illinois, in 1851. At first the town was called Riddlesburg, then Riddles, before they finally settled on Riddle.

Left: Camas Valley was named for the abundance of camas that grow locally. The town was established in 1870.

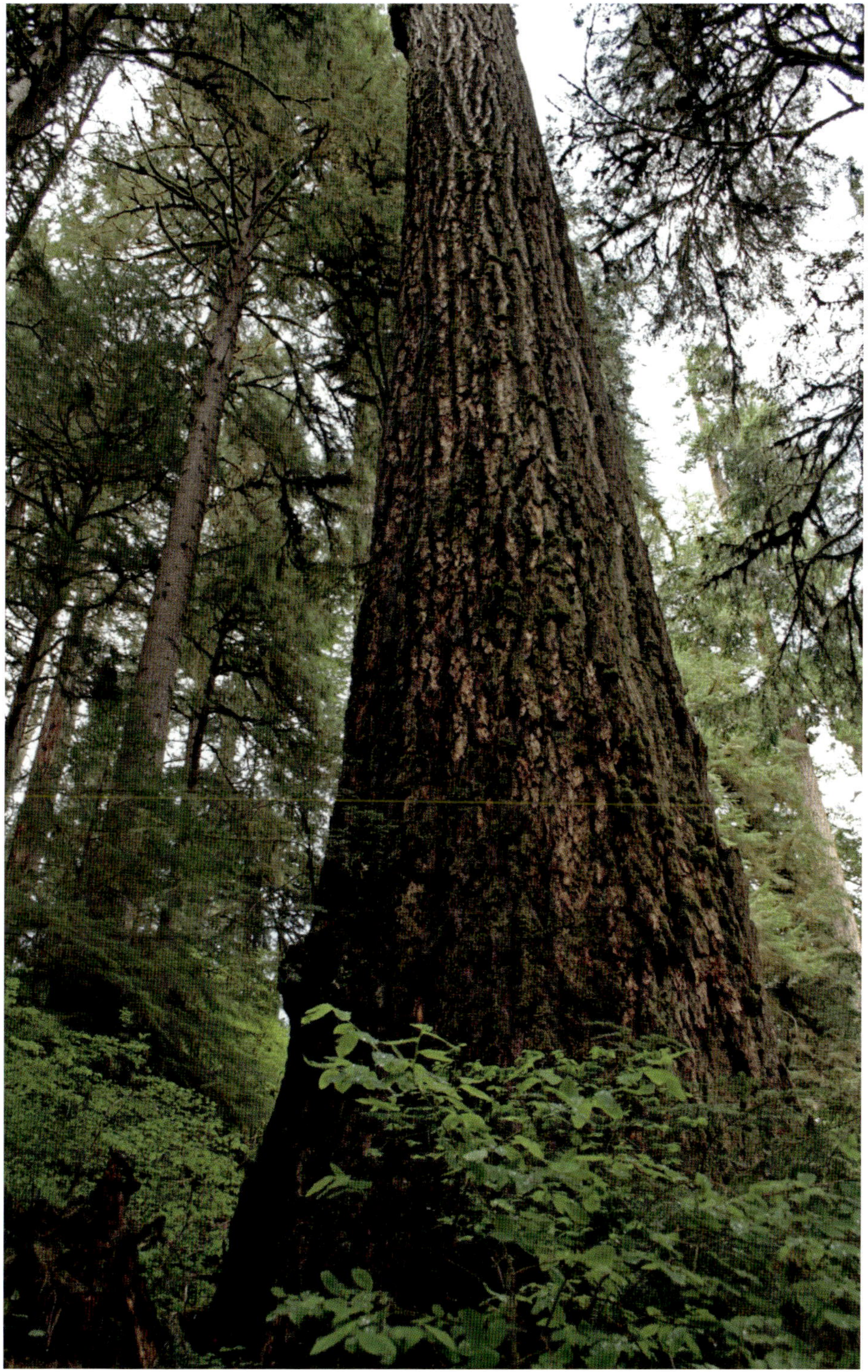

Douglas County has some of the largest sugar pine trees in the United States.

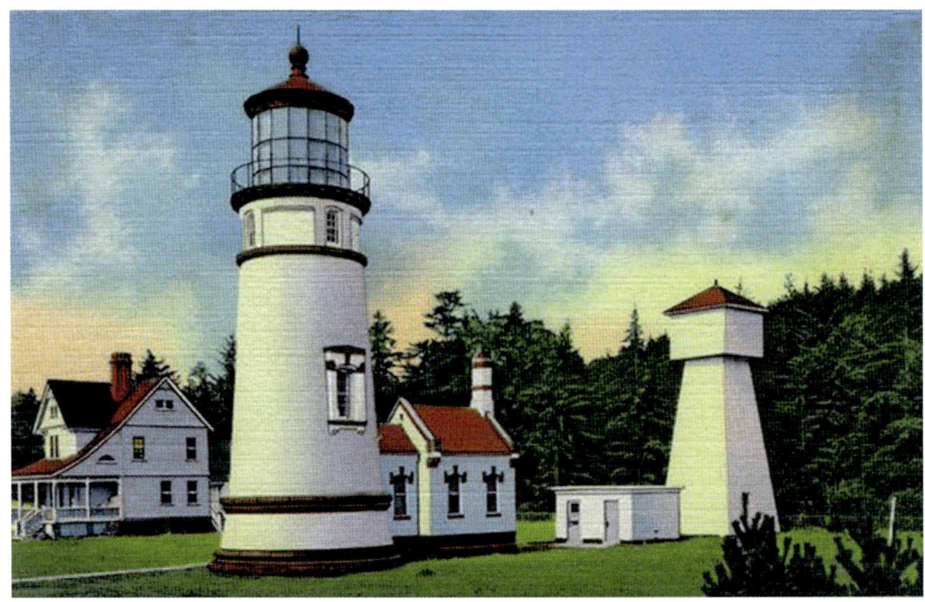

This Umpqua Lighthouse was built in 1890 to replace the original one that was built in 1857. The original lighthouse collapsed after many large storms. The lens for the lighthouse was constructed using 616 glass prisms that were handcrafted in France.

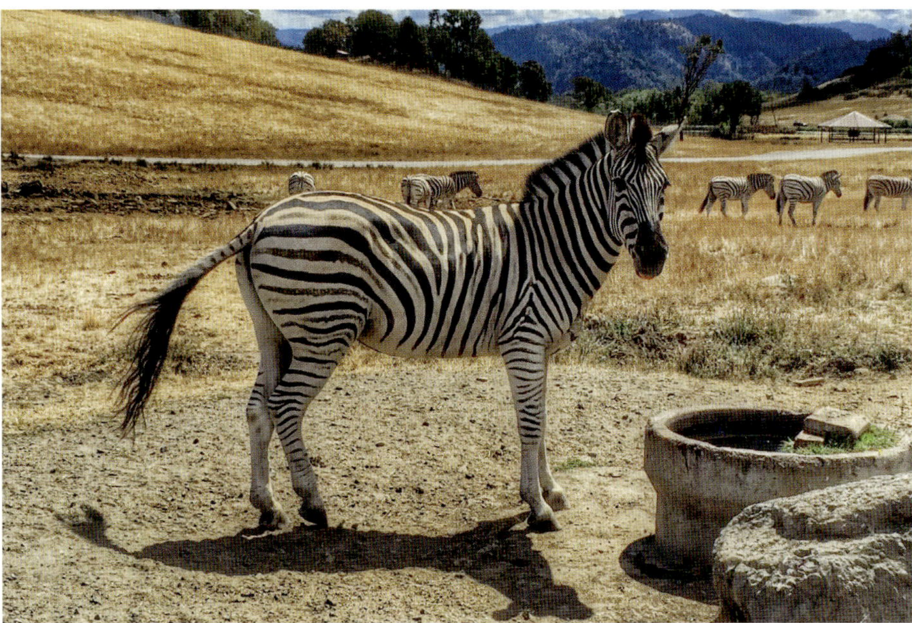

Wildlife Safari in Winston is the only drive-through animal park in Oregon. It is also the number one cheetah breeding facility outside of Africa. Hundreds of animals roam the 600 acres. There is an international veterinary program on site to care for the animals. The animal park was founded in 1972 with the express desire to conserve, educate, and preserve native and exotic wildlife.

4

COOS AND CURRY COUNTIES

Coos County was originally part of Umpqua and Jackson counties. The territorial government created Coos County in 1853. Explorers who came across the Coos Indians used various spellings of the word in their journals.

Curry County was established two years later when the territorial government realigned the counties and took a portion of Coos County to create Curry County. The county was named for George Law Curry, a pioneer from Pennsylvania. Upon arriving in Oregon City, he became the editor of the *Oregon Spectator*. He went on to become the publisher of the *Oregon Free Press*. He represented Clackamas County in the provisional legislature. He also served as the chief clerk of the territorial council. In 1853, President Pierce appointed him to be the secretary of the Territory of Oregon. He was acting territorial governor for a period of time on two different occasions before he was officially appointed the governor of the Oregon Territory. He served in that position until Oregon became a state in 1859.

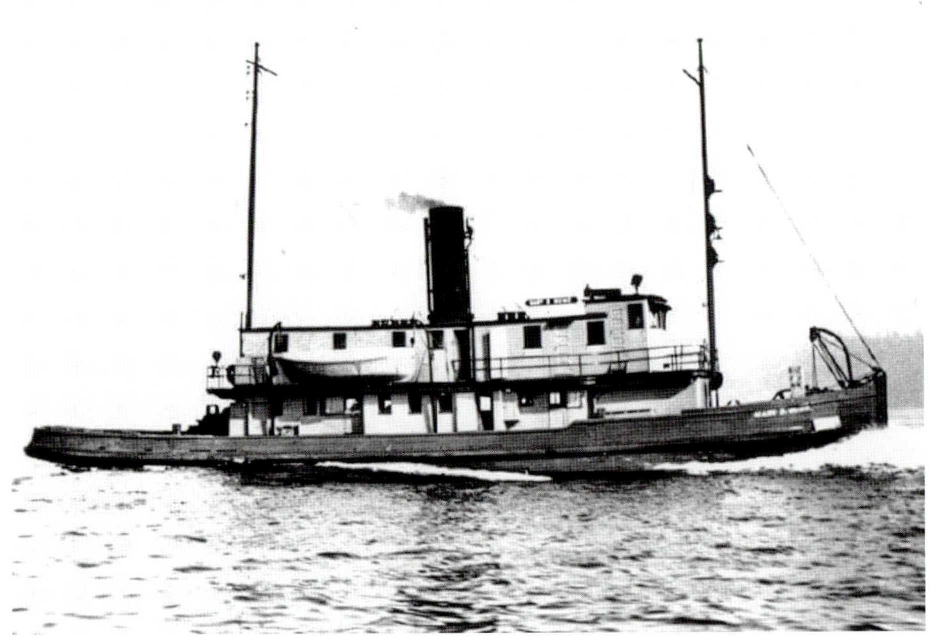

The *Mary D. Hume* ship is pictured. The ship was built on the Rogue River in 1881. R. D. Hume named the ship for his wife, Mary Duncan Hume. During the ship's ninety-seven-year career, she transported goods from Gold Beach to San Francisco, worked as a whaling vessel in the Arctic, as a halibut fishing vessel, and as a tugboat towing logs in Puget Sound.

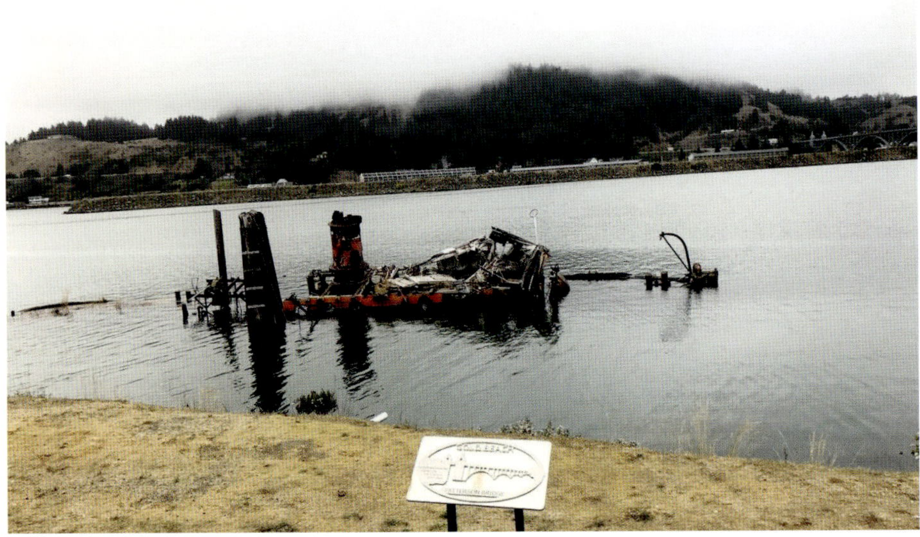

The *Mary D. Hume* returned to Gold Beach in 1978 under her own power. She had a few close calls during her long career, including sinking through ice in Alaska in 1904. Crews were able to raise her out of the ice, and tow her to Seattle where she was repaired. From 1952 until her retirement, she was the oldest commercial vessel on the Pacific Coast. The remains of the ship are pictured.

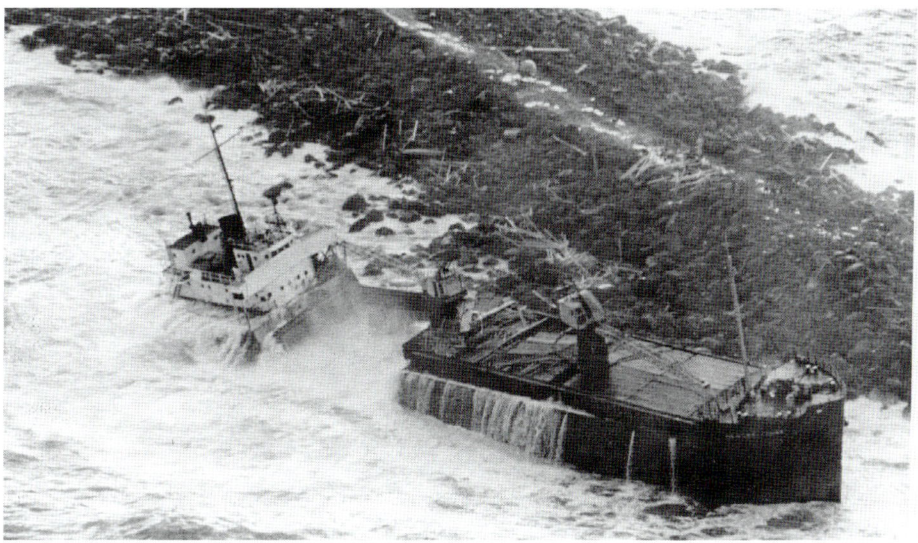

In December 1962, the *Alaska Cedar Lumber Ship* was tossed onto Coos Bay's north jetty during a violent storm. The ship, which measured 256 feet in length, broke into three pieces. All the crew members aboard were rescued by the Coast Guard. Some of the lumber onboard the ship sank into the ocean, and some washed ashore. The ship's insurance carrier posted signs warning that no one was allowed to take the salvaged lumber.

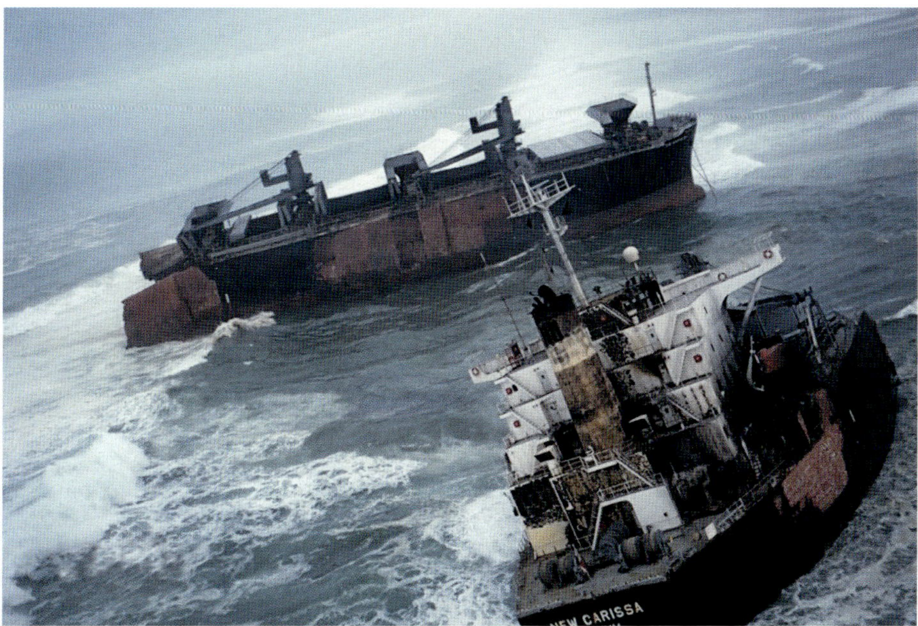

On February 4, 1999, the MV *New Carissa* ran aground north of the entrance to Coos Bay. The ship was 640 feet long and 105 feet wide. It was empty when it approached Coos Bay. The ship was scheduled to pick up a large load of wood chips, which is what the ship was built for. Upon impact, it broke in two. The shipwreck had a devastating impact on the environment and marine life.

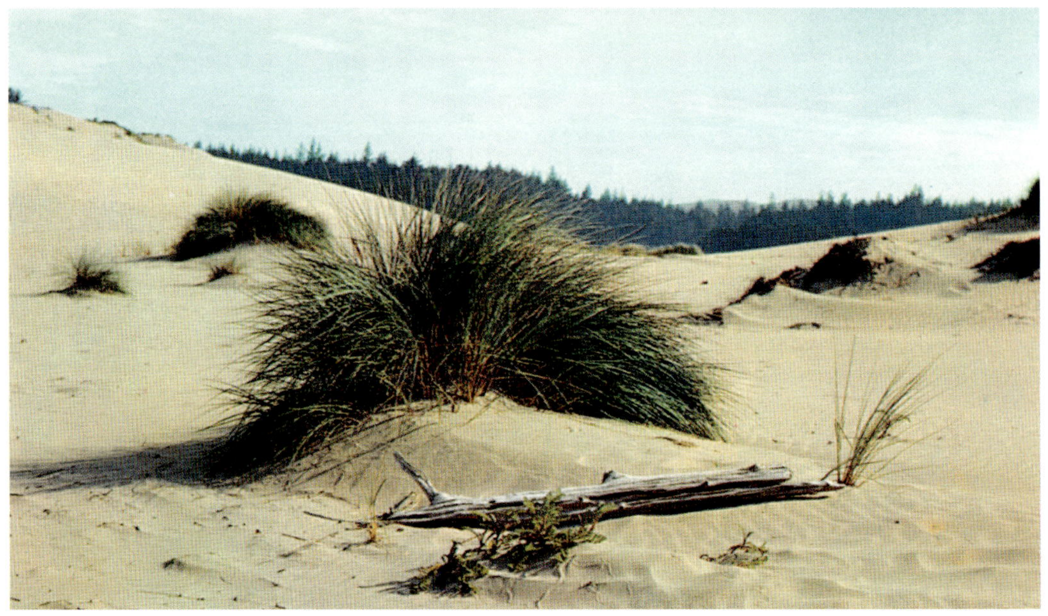

People come from every corner of the globe to enjoy Oregon's sand dunes.

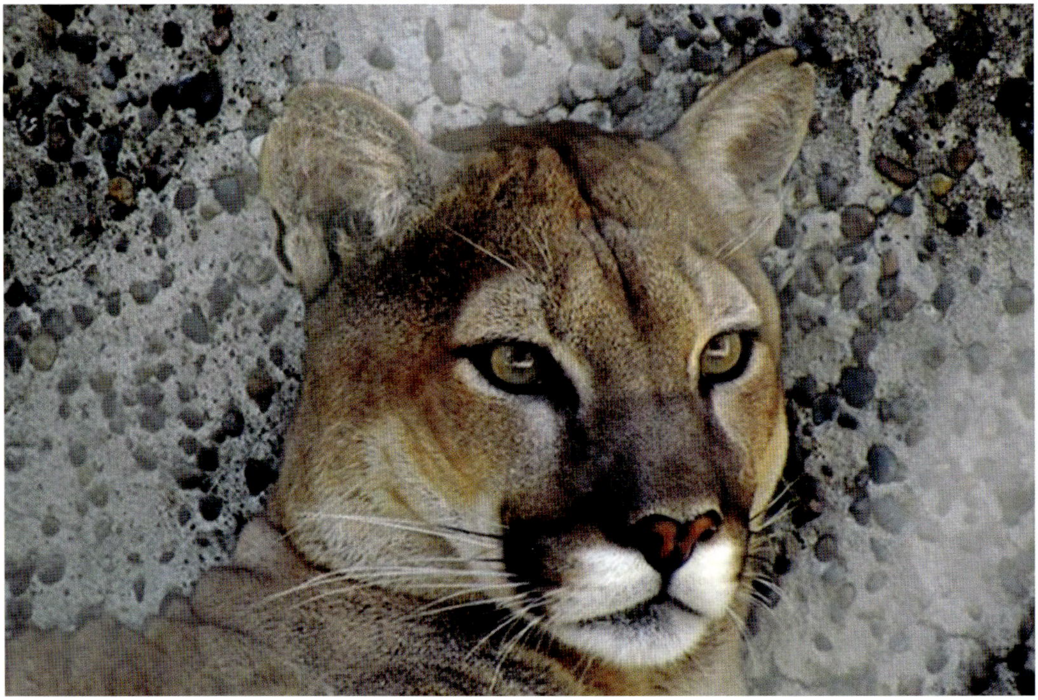

West Coast Game Park Safari is home to hundreds of animals who serve as ambassadors for education relating to conservation and extinction of their species. Many of the animals are free to roam the grounds alongside the visitors.

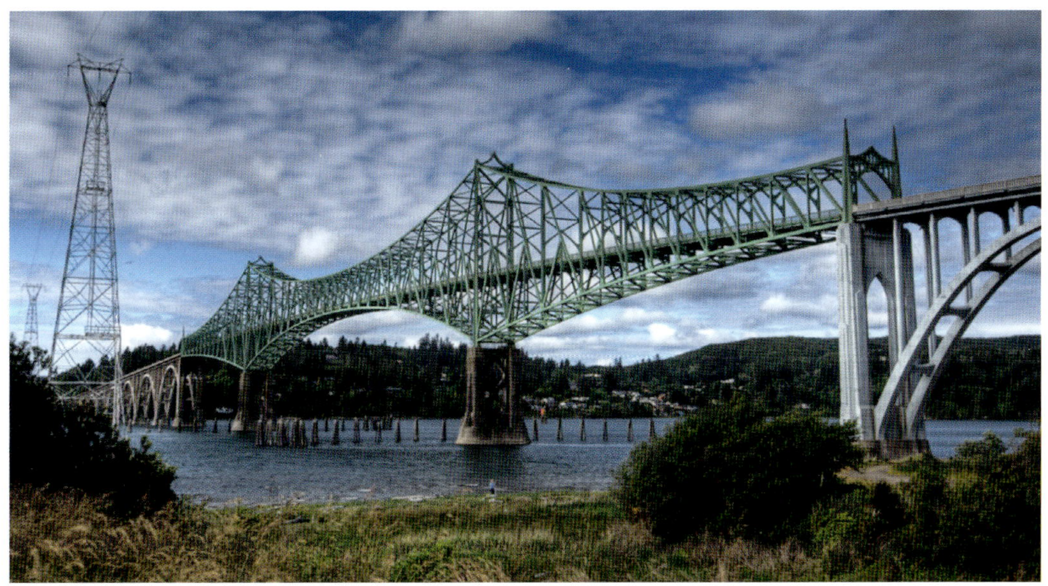

The McCollough Bridge is named for Conde B. McCollough who oversaw the construction of this bridge and ten others in Oregon. The cantilever bridge replaced the ferries that had previously crossed the bay. When the bridge was built in 1936, it cost over two million dollars. It took twelve million pounds of steel, five million board feet of lumber, 48,000 cubic yards of concrete, and 24,000 cubic yards of soil to build the bridge.

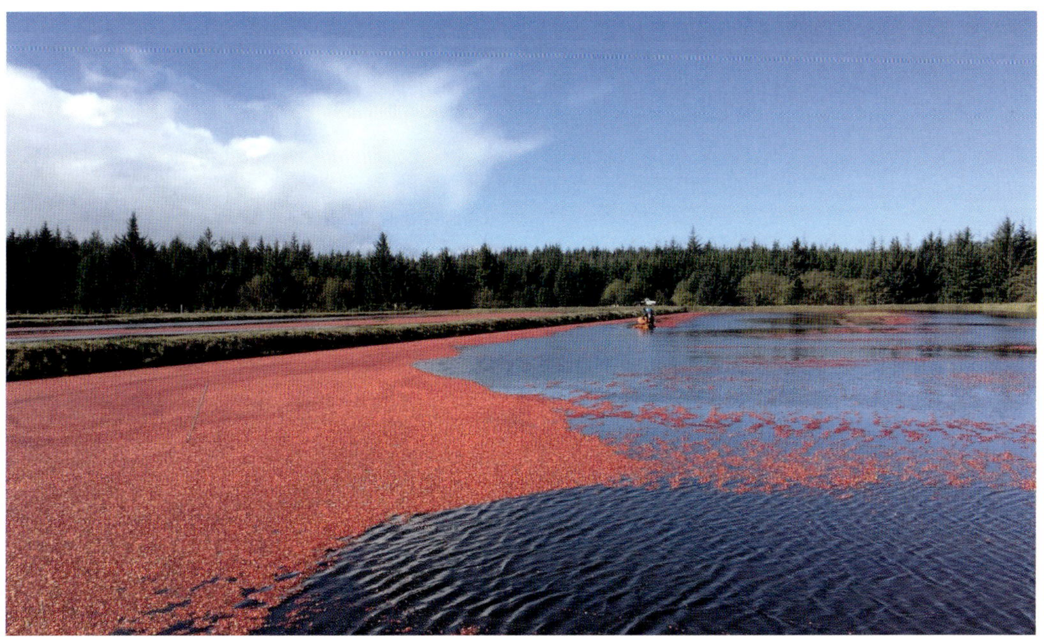

Charles McFarlin is credited with planting the first crop of cranberries in Bandon in 1885. He planted five acres with a wild variety that he brought from Massachusetts.

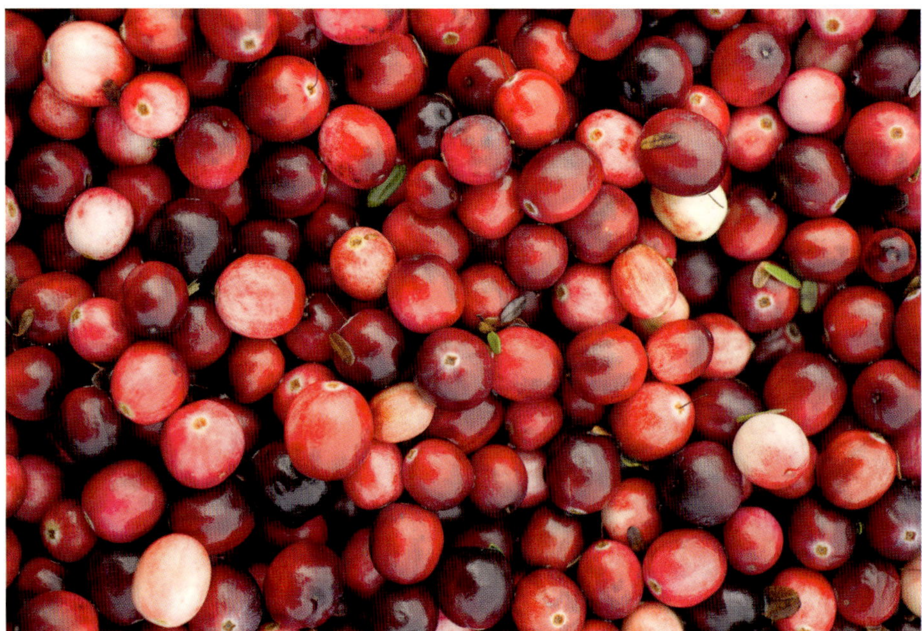

Today, Bandon is known as the "Cranberry Capital of Oregon." Cranberries are grown in other parts of the world, but the United States is the leader. The cranberries grown in Oregon have a longer growing season, which results in a deeper color than cranberries grown elsewhere.

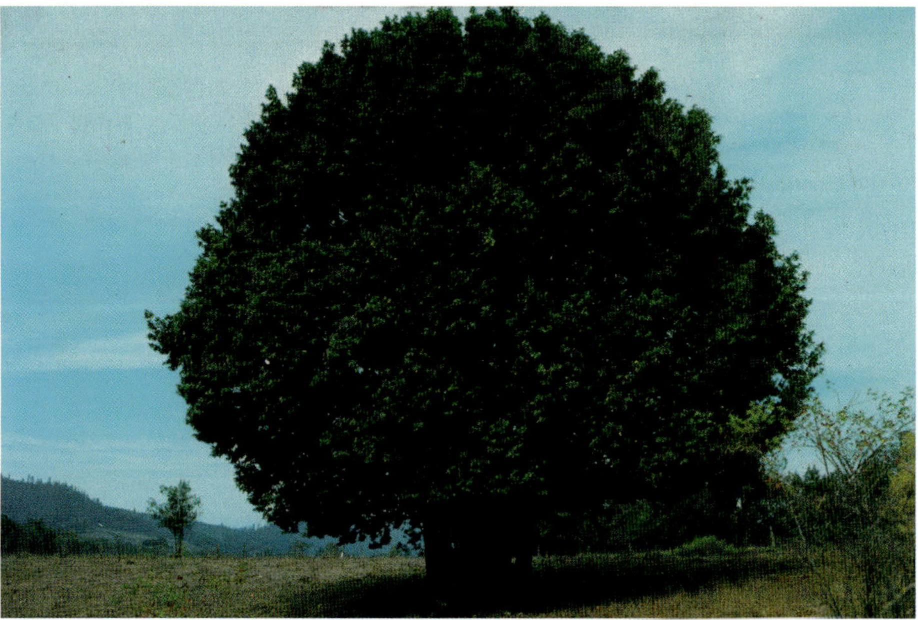

There are very few places in the world where Myrtlewood trees grow. They are known to grow in Jerusalem, along the Oregon and California coasts, and in the Sierra foothills in California.

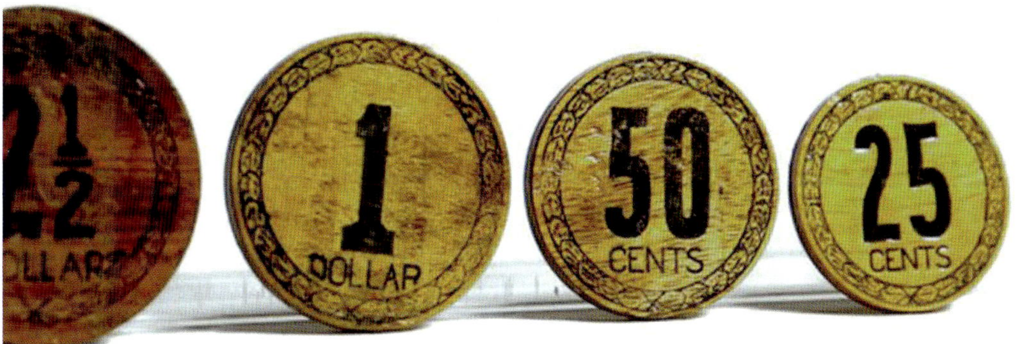

They say that money doesn't grow on trees, but residents of North Bend, Oregon, may beg to differ. During the Great Depression, the only bank in town closed its doors. The North Bend City Council authorized $1,000 to be printed on discs of Myrtlewood and used to cover the city's payroll. When the local bank reopened, the city asked that people turn in their Myrtlewood money. Many chose to keep it as a souvenir.

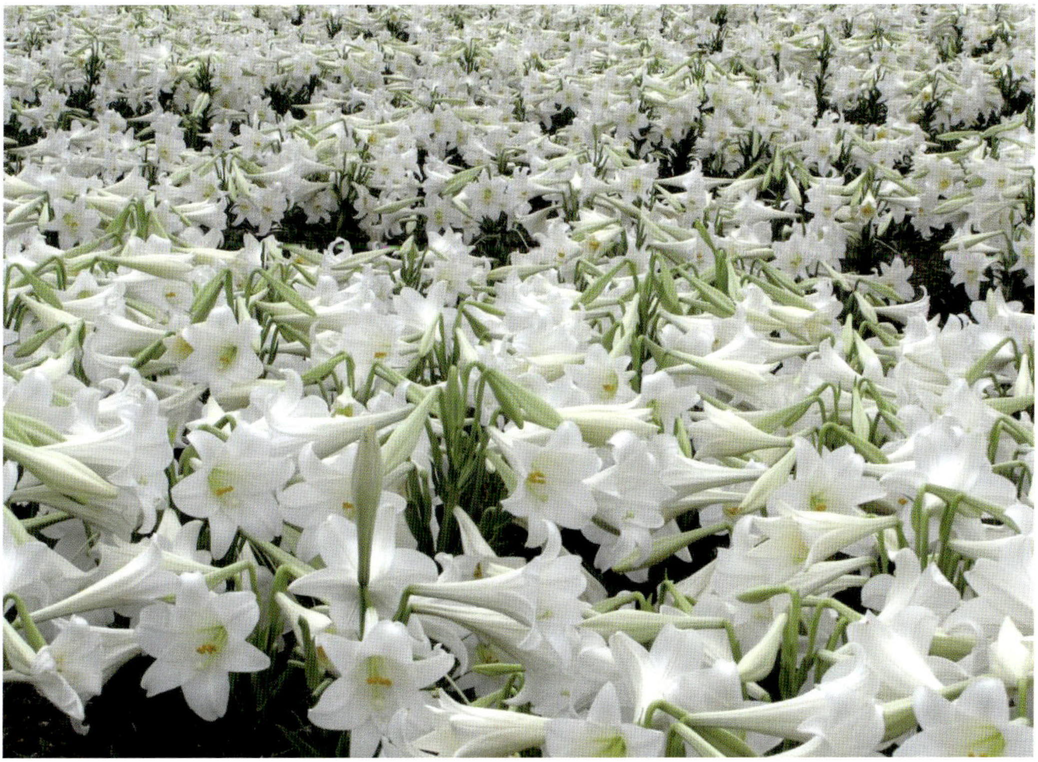

Today, Brookings is well known for their beautiful Easter lilies. This began when Louis Houghton arrived in town with a suitcase of hybrid lily bulbs. He had recently retired from the U.S. Department of Agriculture and believed that the lilies would grow well in Brookings. He gave away the bulbs to anyone interested in planting them. There wasn't much interest in the beginning, but over the years the crops gained in popularity.

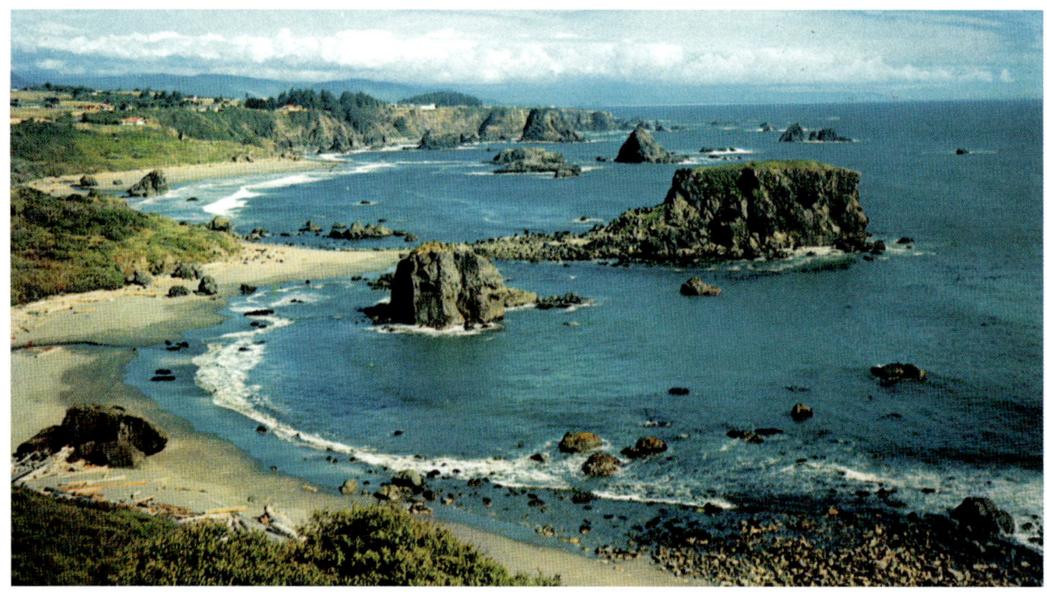

This vintage postcard shows the Harris Beach State Park. The park was named after pioneer George Scott Harris. He was born in Scotland in 1836. He served in the British Army in India, Africa, and New Zealand. He arrived in San Francisco in 1860 and worked in mining and on the railroads. In 1871, he came to Curry County and raised sheep and cattle on what is now Harris Beach State Park.

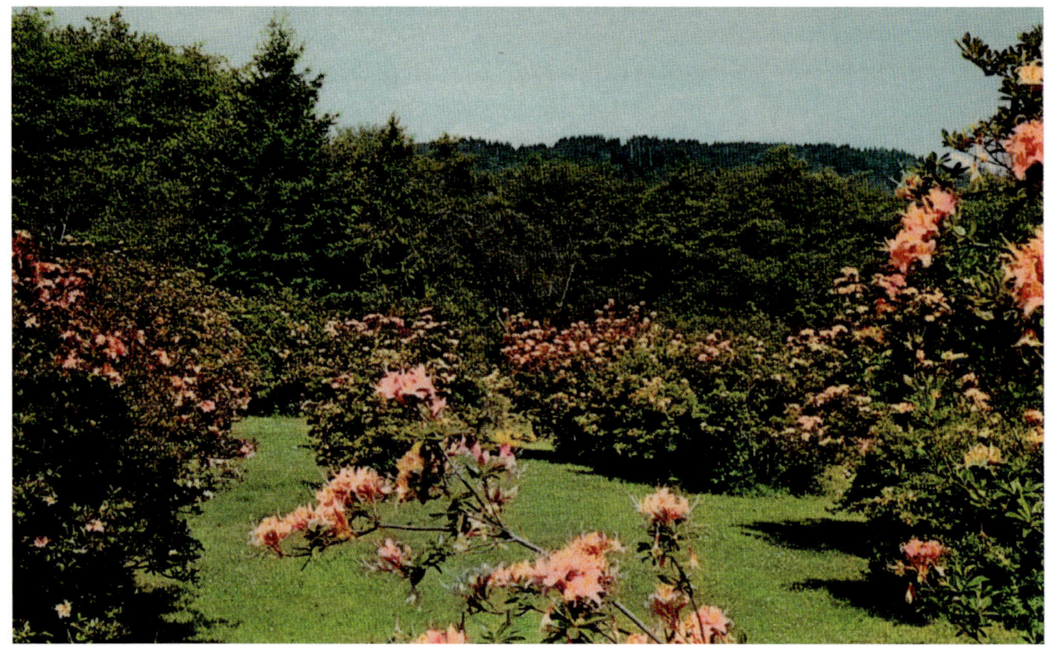

The Azalea State Park was dedicated on May 20, 1939. Arch B. Sanders of the Highway Association made an 8-millimeter color film of the park's dedication ceremony. Color film was still a novelty at the time, so he used it to promote the Oregon coast.

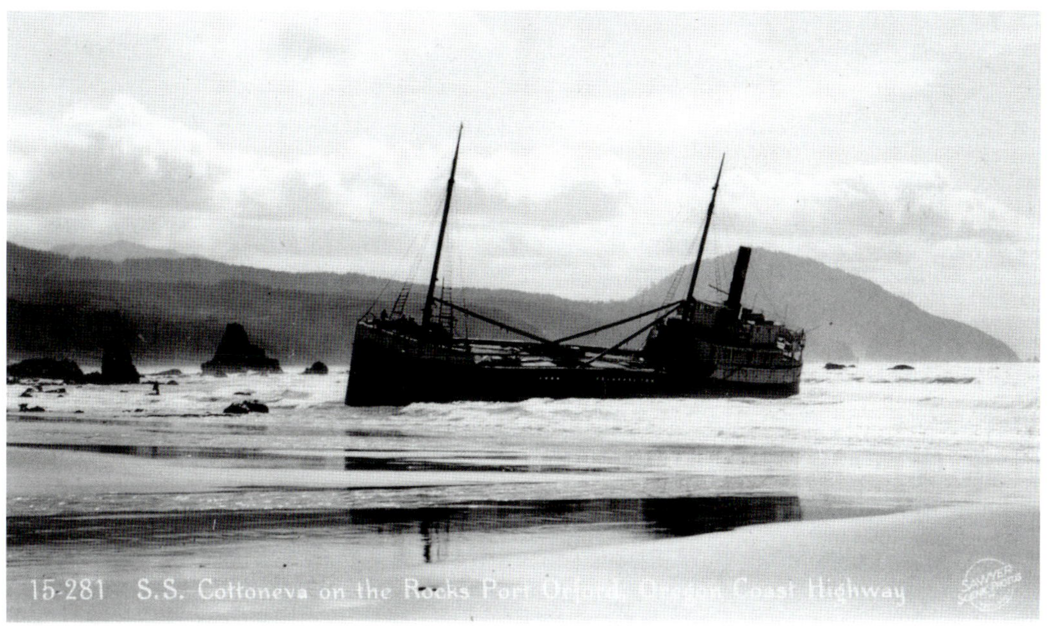

In 1937, there was a shipping strike in Port Orford. The Trans-Pacific Lumber Company had amassed a tremendous amount of product that needed to be shipped out. In February the SS *Cottoneva* docked at Port Orford with the plan to load the lumber. The next day, gusts of wind came up and the SS *Cottoneva* was pushed ashore and later went aground. The entire crew was rescued.

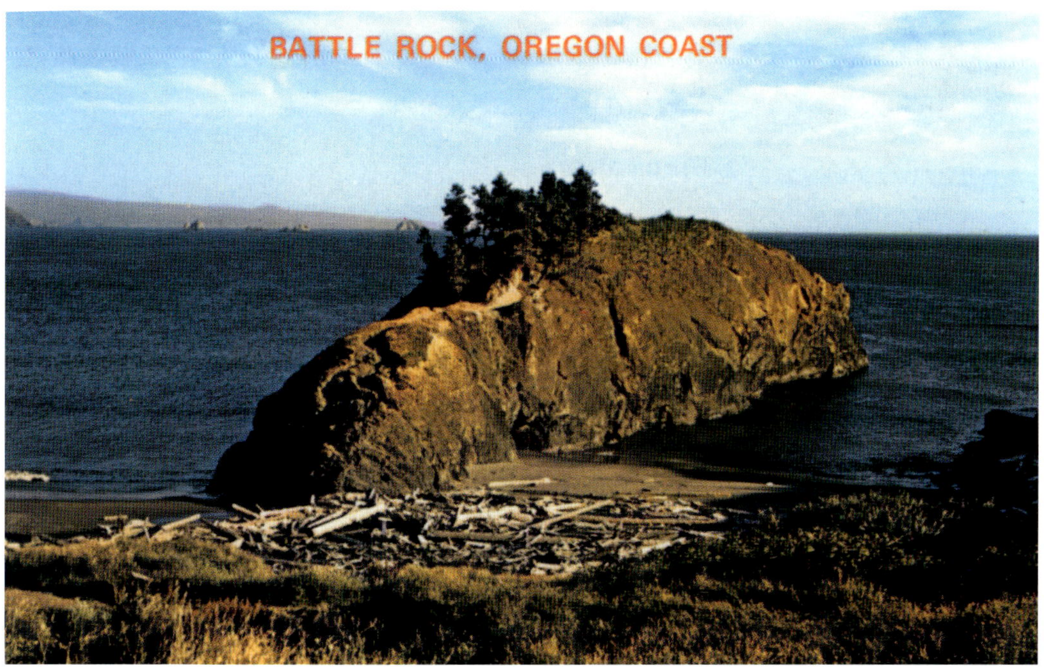

Battle Rock was named for a battle that took place between the pioneers and the Indians in 1851.

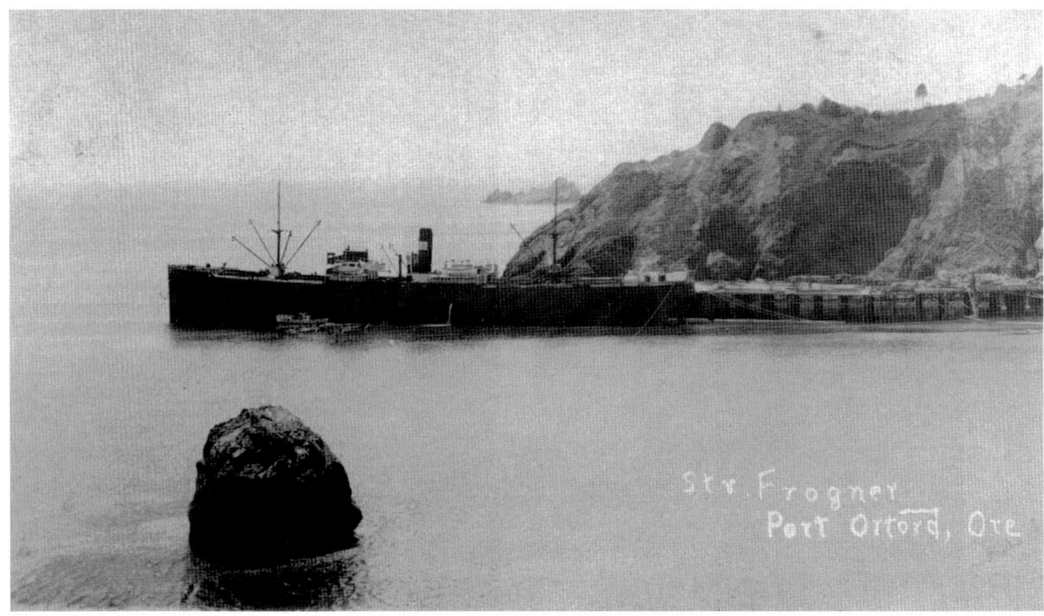

The largest ship that ever docked at Port Orford was the SS *Frogner*. It measured 407 feet in length. The SS *Frogner* was built in 1921 in Great Britain. She docked at Port Orford in 1925 and loaded logs to haul to Japan. In 1926, the ship was sold to a company based in Spain. The *Frogner* was hit by an Italian submarine and sank in the Strait of Gibraltar during World War II.

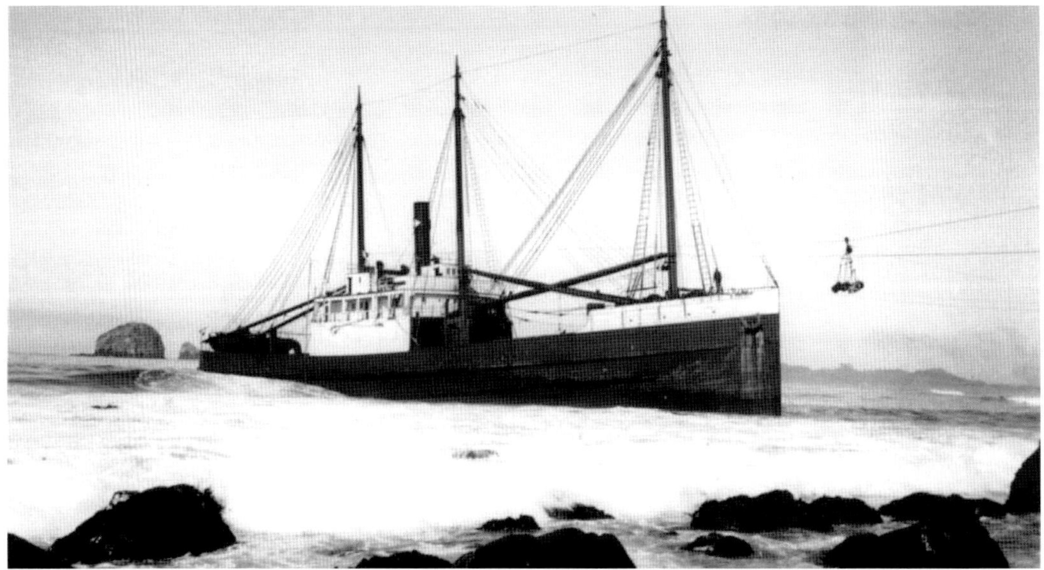

The *Phyllis* struck a submerged rock off the beach near Humbug Mountain during a winter storm in 1936. The *Phyllis* was a 1,266-ton steam vessel that was built in 1917. She was carrying 400 tons of general cargo. She was enroute to Portland from San Francisco. Captain Victory Jacobsen and all twenty-two crew members were rescued by the Coast Guard.

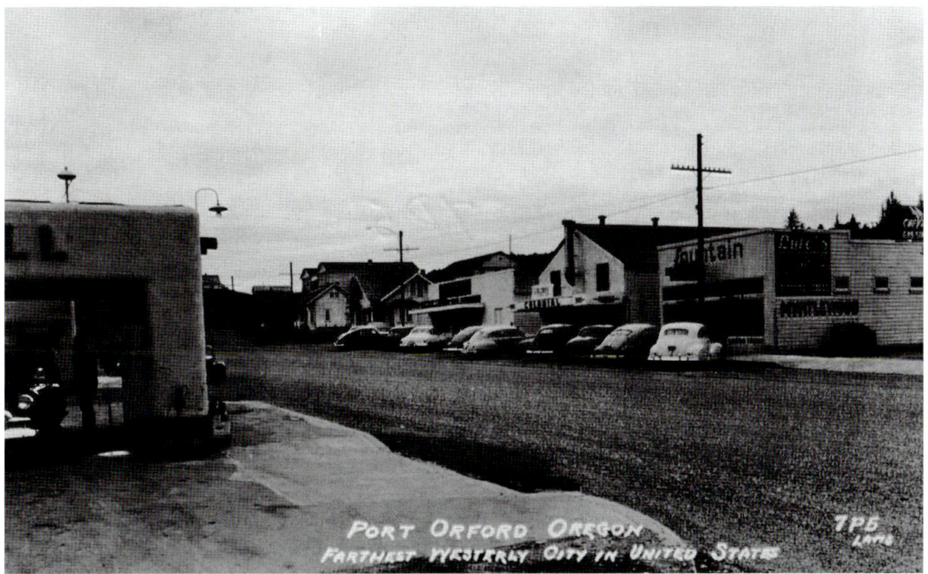

Port Orford is the furthest western city in the United States. It was founded in 1856 and quickly became an important port for shipping lumber.

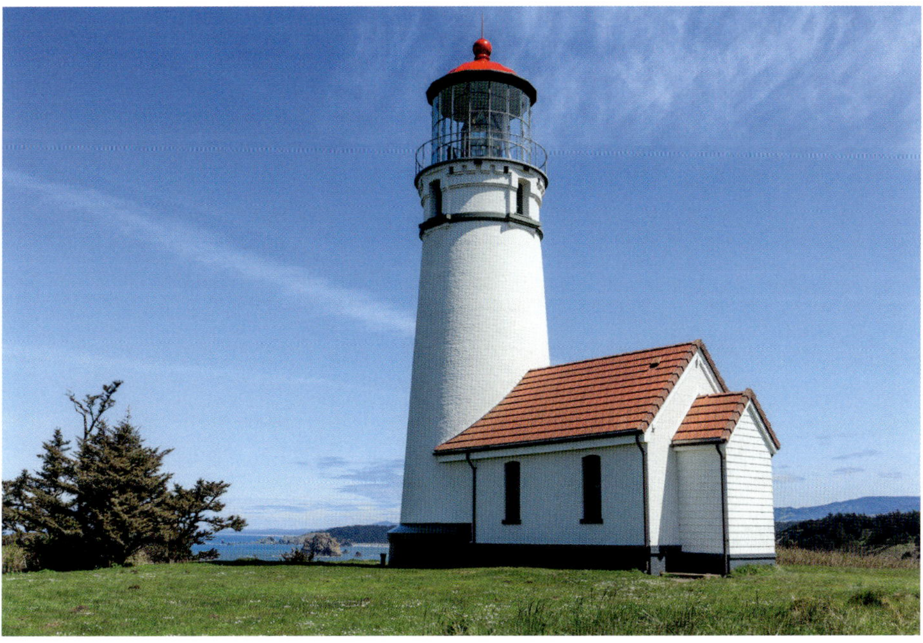

The Cape Blanco Lighthouse began operating in 1870. It is the oldest continually operating lighthouse in Oregon. Its focal point is taller, and it is located further west than any lighthouse in Oregon. The Cape Blanco Lighthouse hired the first female lighthouse keeper in Oregon, Mabel Bretherton. She began her career in 1903 after her husband died. He had been a lighthouse keeper at the Coquille Lighthouse. Mabel and her three children kept watch over the sea.

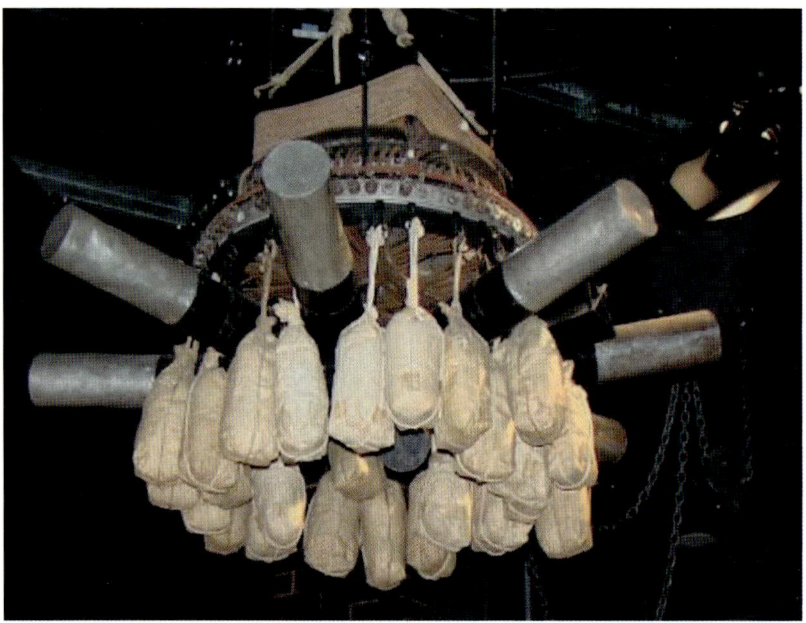

On the morning of September 9, 1942, the U.S. Forest Service heard a plane overhead near Brookings. It flew a short distance into the forest, then retreated quickly. A Forest Service employee fired at the plane with unknown results. Soon after, a fire was detected near Mount Emily. The plane had come off a Japanese submarine located off shore and dropped an incendiary bomb. The fire was put out and there were no injuries.

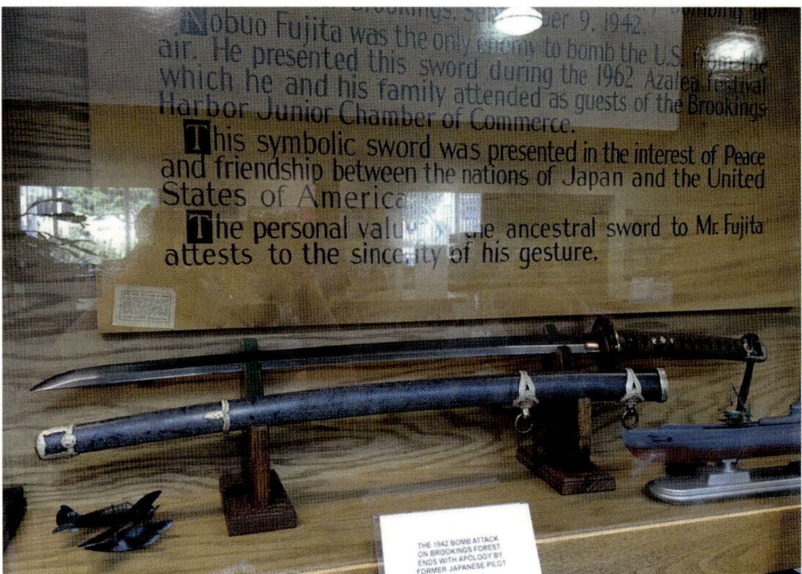

Twenty years later, the pilot of that plane, Nubuo Fujita, returned to Brookings through an international goodwill project. He presented a 500-year-old Samurai sword to the City of Brookings as a gesture of goodwill and peace between the two nations.